GCSE Exam Secrets

Information and Communication Technology

Steve Cushing

CONTENTS

To revise any of these topics more thoroughly, see *Letts Revise GCSE ICT Study Guide*

(see inside back cover for how to order)

THIS BOOK AND YOUR GCSE EXAMS

Introduction

This book is designed to help you get better results.

▶ Look at the grade A and C candidates' answers and see if you could have done better.

▶ Try the exam practice questions and then look at the answers.

▶ Make sure you understand why the answers given are correct.

▶ When you feel ready, try the GCSE mock exam papers.

If you perform well on the questions in this book you should do well in the examination. Remember that success in examinations is about hard work, not luck.

What examiners look for

▶ Examiners are obviously looking for the right answer, however, it does not have to match the wording in the examiner's marking scheme exactly.

▶ Your answer will be marked correct if the answer is a correct ICT answer, even if it is not expressed exactly as it is on the mark scheme.

▶ Use of the correct terms is very important in ICT examinations, but examiners do not give marks for naming specific software. You should use terms like spreadsheet, not Excel.

▶ The examiner has to use professional judgement to interpret your answers, but will be looking for key words and phrases.

▶ You do not get extra marks for writing a lot of irrelevant words. The number of lines allowed gives you an indication of how much you are expected to write.

▶ You should make sure that your answer is clear, easy to read and concise.

▶ You must make sure that your diagrams are neatly drawn. You do not need to use a ruler to draw diagrams. They are often drawn too small for the examiner to see them clearly. They should be clearly labelled with label lines.

▶ On some papers, you will need to draw system flow charts. Draw these clearly and remember that you will be marked on the accuracy and sequence of the charts.

Exam technique

▶ You should spend the first few minutes of the assessment reading through the whole question paper.

▶ Use the mark allocation to guide you on how many points you need to make and how much to write.

▶ You should aim to use one minute for each mark; thus if a question has 5 marks, it should take you 5 minutes to answer the question.

▶ Plan your answers; do not write down the first thing that comes into your head. Planning is absolutely necessary in questions requiring continuous and extended answer questions.

▶ Do not plan to have time left over at the end. If you do use it usefully. Check you have answered all the questions, check arithmetic and read longer answers to make sure you have not made silly mistakes or missed things out.

DIFFERENT TYPES OF QUESTIONS

Different types of questions

ICT GCSE examinations have 40% of the marks allocated to externally set and marked examination papers or tasks. The only exception to this are the Double Award GCSEs, which can have as little as 15% externally set and marked examinations or tasks. Your ICT examination is likely to have one, two or three set examination papers.

Two types of questions are used in ICT examinations. Some questions ask you to state one word answers, or select from a range of choices given. This type of question aims to test your breadth of knowledge. These questions are referred to as short answer questions, or, where you have a choice, as multiple choice questions. Examination papers in ICT often start with this type of question, or for those of you taking a full course GCSE in ICT, your first examination paper may totally consist of this type of question. The other type of question requires extended writing, where you are normally expected to write more than two sentences linked together on a topic. Candidates often do less well on this type of question as they fail to include enough relevant scoring points. You will notice in this book how examiners often look for the number of aspects or points outlined in the mark scheme. When you answer this type of question, you must try to include the relevant number of points.

Sometimes, extended writing questions are structured into sub-sections. These sections are often written with what is called a ramp of difficulty. This simply means that the first part of the question is easy. The next part is slightly more difficult, and the last part is the most difficult. Often, the last part of the question is used to determine Grade A candidates. You should work through these ramped questions, section by section, but remember that you do not have to get each part right before you tackle the next part. Most extended writing questions start with what is called a stem. This stem is an introductory statement which aims to provide much of the information you will need to answer the question.

- Make sure you read and understand the stem before you tackle the question.

- Keep referring back to the stem as it will contain clues to the answers to parts of the question.

- Remember that the examiner will only include in the stem information that is required to answer the question.

WHAT MAKES AN A/A*, B OR C GRADE CANDIDATE

GRADE A* ANSWER

The specification identifies what an A, C and F candidate can do in general terms. Examiners have to interpret these criteria when they fix grade boundaries. Boundaries are not a fixed mark every year and there is not a fixed percentage who achieve a grade each year. Boundaries are fixed by looking at candidates' work and comparing the standards with candidates of previous years. If the paper is harder than usual the boundary mark will go down. The A* boundary has no criteria but is fixed initially as the same mark above the A boundary as the B is below it.

GRADE A ANSWER

A grade candidates have a wide knowledge of ICT and can apply that knowledge to new situations. An A grade candidate generally has no bad questions and scores marks throughout. An A grade candidate has to have sat Higher tier papers. The minimum percentage for an A grade candidate is about 80%.

GRADE B ANSWER

B grade candidates will have a reasonable knowledge of the topics identified as Higher tier only. The minimum percentage for a B candidate is exactly halfway between the minimum for A and C (on Higher tier).

GRADE C ANSWER

C grade candidates can get their grade either by taking Higher tier papers or by taking Foundation tier papers. There are some questions common to both papers and these are aimed at C and D candidates. The minimum percentage for a C on Foundation tier is approximately 65% but on Higher tier it is approximately 45%.

HOW TO BOOST YOUR GRADE

Grade booster ⋯⋯▶ How to turn C into B

▸ All marks have the same value. Don't forget the easy marks are just as important as the hard ones. Learn the definitions – these are easy marks in exams and they reward effort and good preparation. If you want to boost your grade, you cannot afford to miss out on these marks – they are easier to get.

▸ Look carefully at the command word at the start of the sentence. Make sure you understand what is required when the word is **state**, **suggest**, **describe**, **explain** etc.

▸ Try to answer all of the questions and make the right number of relevant points.

▸ Do not use specific software names.

▸ If the question asks you to write about the use of an example of ICT, you should describe how the function is used. Don't just name a type of software, such as a database.

▸ Underline the key points made in the question and make sure that you cover them fully in your answer.

▸ Make sure that the examiner can read your answer. You will not get marks, however correct your answer, if the examiner cannot read it.

▸ Do not repeat answers that you have already given earlier in the question or examination paper. Papers are carefully structured to ensure that the same answer is not asked for twice.

Grade booster ⋯⋯▶ How to turn B into A/A*

▸ In questions requiring extended writing make sure you make enough good points and you don't miss out important points. Read the answer through and correct any spelling, punctuation and grammar mistakes.

▸ Always use correct technical terms.

▸ Try to give examples of use in extended writing questions.

▸ Remember that the examiner is looking for your breadth and depth of knowledge.

▸ At Grade A, examiners are looking for some imagination and originality.

CHAPTER 1

Information systems and hardware

To revise this topic more thoroughly, see Chapters 1 and 2 in *Letts Revise GCSE Information and Communication Technology Study Guide.*

 Try this sample GCSE question and then compare your answer with the Grade C and Grade A model answers on pages 10 and 11.

a   Explain and describe the term information system.

....

....

....

.... **[4]**

b   State the name and function of a device that could be used at each stage of the following diagram of an information system.

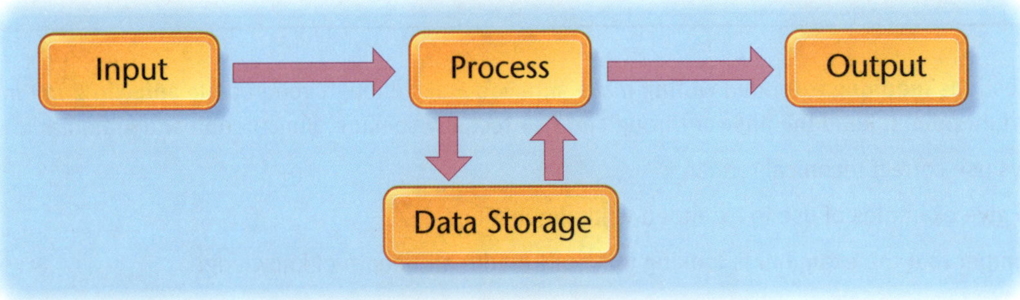

	Device	Function
Input		
Process		
Data storage		
Output		

[8]

c Representation of data within information systems.

Complete the table below, adding definitions for the terms.

Term	Definition
Digital	
Analogue	
Bit	
Byte	
Kilobyte	
Megabyte	

[12]

d Describe the purpose of the **microprocessor** in a dishwasher.

....

....

....

....

....

....

....

[8]

(Total 32 marks)

GRADE C ANSWER

Robert has mentioned the use of computers and linking but has not shown any real understanding of the system. To gain higher marks he should mention input, process and output.

Robert has answered in simple terms. Where the answer is appropriate, marks are awarded. Where the answer requires more detailed information, the mark is not awarded. There are four boxes to complete and eight marks. The examiner is looking for more than a single word answer in the function box.

Robert has shown a limited understanding of the terms. Again, look at the allocated marks and give a detailed response.

Five marks would be awarded: one for the processor being used to control the appliance; one for linking it correctly to the appliance; one for mentioning different types of wash; one for putting them in a sequence; one for mentioning switching on and off of pumps and motors.

To gain more marks you will have to describe how the microprocessor can be pre-programmed to perform a dedicated task that is required by the washing machine. Marks are awarded for linking the device to its purpose.

ROBERT

a A computer and a modem linked to the Internet is an information system. ✓ You input data using a keyboard. ✓

b

	Device	Function
Input	Keyboard ✓	Type in data ✓
Process	CPU	Carries out calculations ✓
Data storage	Disk	Holds information
Output	VDU ✓	Shows output on screen

c

Term	Definition	mark
Digital	Like a watch showing only numbers ✓	1
Analogue	Like a clock, with hands ✓	1
Bit	A small amount of data ✓	1
Byte	8 bits ✓	1
Kilobyte	1000 bits	
Megabyte	1 000 000 bits	

d The dishwasher has to perform a number of different types of wash with activities in a certain order. ✓ The microprocessor switches the pumps ✓ and motors ✓ on and off in the correct sequence. ✓

15 marks = Grade C answer

Grade booster ⋯> move a C to a B

To gain higher marks you need to write full answers. Look at the number of marks available and then make one point in your answer for each mark.

GRADE A ANSWER

Zeena has shown a clear understanding of the term and used technical language to complete the description. Four marks awarded.

Zeena has given an appropriate device and well-described function for each aspect of the system but has given a one-word answer for the output function. Visual display on a screen would have gained the extra mark. The examiner is looking for more than a single word answer in the function box. Seven marks awarded.

Zeena has shown a clear understanding of the terms and was able to supply clear definitions. The definitions of kilobyte and megabyte contain incorrect figures, but using the word approximately makes the answer acceptable. Twelve marks awarded.

Eight marks would be awarded: one for mentioning correct terminology in embedded systems; one for the processor being used to control the appliance; one for linking it correctly to the appliance; one for mentioning different types of wash; one for mentioning ability to pre-program; one for mentioning sequence; one for mentioning reliability; one for ability to upgrade/contrasting with other traditional methods of controlling sequences. To get full marks you must give examples of use contrasting a microprocessor-controlled dish-washing machine with other traditional methods of controlling sequences.

ZEENA

a The flow of data from input, ✓ into a control area ✓ with some form of feedback, ✓ before being sent to an output ✓ point is an information system.

b

	Device	
Input	Keyboard/mouse ✓	Type in data/move curser or pointing device ✓
Process	Arithmetic unit ✓	Carries out calculations on the data input ✓
Data storage	magnetic disk	Stores information for later use in digital format on magnetic surface of disk ✓
Output	Monitor ✓	Visually

c

Term	Definition	mark
Digital	Data ✓ supplied in 1s and 0s only ✓	2
Analogue	Data ✓ supplied in a range of different states ✓	2
Bit	A single data entry ✓ (binary digit) ✓	2
Byte	A group ✓ of 8 bits ✓	2
Kilobyte	Approximately 1000 bytes, 8000 bits ✓✓	2
Megabyte	Approximately 1 000 000 bytes, 8 000 000 bits ✓	2

d A dishwasher uses an embedded system ✓ that is pre-programmed to perform the dedicated tasks required for the various wash cycles. ✓ Embedded systems are smaller ✓ and more reliable ✓ than traditional motor- or clockwork-driven control systems. Precise timings ✓ for pump and motor actions can be controlled by the microprocessor. It is even possible to re-program ✓ the microprocessor to cope with advances in washing powder technology. ✓

31 marks = Grade A answer

QUESTION BANK

Short-answer questions

1 What hardware do you need in order to make full use of a word processor?

A CD-ROM, printer and keyboard

B keyboard, monitor and printer

C monitor, keyboard and mouse

D ZIP drive, keyboard and mouse. ①

2 An information system can be described as:

A inputs, storage, processing, outputs and feedback

B computer monitor, mouse and keyboard

C modem

D an electronic conversation between two people. ①

3 Which of the following is a piece of information?

A Steve has a blue car

B blue

C car

D Northamptonshire ①

4 The various devices that make up a computer system are called:

A Software

B Parts

C Peripherals

D Hardware. ①

5 Which of the following computer systems are made to be portable?

A desktop computer

B laptop computer

C personal digital assistant

D tower computer

E mainframe computer

F palmtop computer ①

6 A modern central heating system contains:

A a dedicated microchip

B a hard drive

C a speaker

D a dual processor. ①

Long-answer questions

1 Henrietta Burgher wishes to purchase a new computer. She sees the following advertisement in a newspaper.

Computer for sale:

17 inch monitor
128mb RAM
40GB hard disk
1.7 gigahertz processor (CPU)
Graphical user interface
Operating system
Ink-jet printer

a) What is the name of the device used to store the data inside the computer?

.... ①

b) Name **two** other devices that Henrietta could use to store data on.

Device 1 .... ①

Device 2 .... ①

c) Describe the main functions of the CPU.

....

....

.... ③

d) Why is **RAM** data described as **volatile**?

....

.... ②

e) What is meant by graphical user interface?

....

.... ②

f) State **one benefit** and **one drawback** of a graphical user interface operating system.

Benefit .... ①

Drawback.. ①

g) State **one benefit** and **one drawback** of using an ink-jet printer.

Benefit .... ①

Drawback.. ①

TOTAL 14

2 A floor turtle is controlled using the following instructions.

forward	n	move	n	centimetres forward
backward	n	move	n	centimetres backwards
turn left	t	turn left	t	degrees
turn right	t	turn right	t	degrees
pen down		place the pen on the paper		
pen up		lift the pen off the paper		

Write down a set of instructions to make the turtle draw a square with sides of 50 cm.

....

....

....

....

....

....

.... ⑨

TOTAL 9

3 Name **two** control devices that can be used in a cooker.

Device 1 .... ①

Device 2 .... ①

TOTAL 2

4 A warehouse uses robotic equipment to transport goods around the warehouse.
Name **one** sensor that could be used to prevent the robot from bumping into people.

.... ①

TOTAL 1

5 An information system is used to count the number of cars entering and leaving
a car park. Data is gained via two infrared beams.

a) Explain how the information system can use the infrared beams to count the number
of cars entering and leaving the car park.

.... ②

b) The car park attendant regularly checks the system to make sure that it works correctly.
Describe **two** tests that he could carry out.

Test 1 .... ①

Test 2 .... ①

c) Having checked the system, the car park attendant is satisfied that it is working
correctly. However, drivers keep complaining that, having entered the car park, they
find there is no parking space. Describe **two limitations** in the design of this information
system that could allow this to happen, and how these limitations could be corrected.

....

....

....

.... ④

TOTAL 8

6 A school is thinking of buying 30 laptop computers instead of building a new
network computer room with 30 personal computers (PCs).

a) State **one** difference between a personal computer and a laptop computer.

.... ①

b) What are the benefits of buying laptop computers rather than building the computer room?

....

....

.... ③

c) What are the drawbacks of buying laptops instead of building a computer room?

....

....

.... ③

TOTAL 7

7 A shop has recently introduced new technology in its main office. The shop uses standard computer systems, but does not have a network.

a) Name **two** input devices that will form part of every work station.

Device 1 .... ①

Device 2 .... ①

b) Name **two** output devices that will form part of every work station.

Device 1 .... ①

Device 2 .... ①

TOTAL 4

8 For each of the devices shown below, state whether the device is:

- an input device
- an output device
- a storage device.

Device	Input	Output	Storage
Mouse			
Light pen			
Printer			
Magnetic tape			
Hard disk			
Hand-held scanner			
Flat screen monitor			
Plotter			
Digital camera			
Zip disk			

9 Look at the objects below. Place the correct letter under each object from the word list.

A plotter

B mainframe computer

C laptop computer

D printer

E mouse

F CD-ROM

G keyboard

H video card

I monitor

J joystick

④

TOTAL 4

10 The illustration shows a computer and its peripherals.

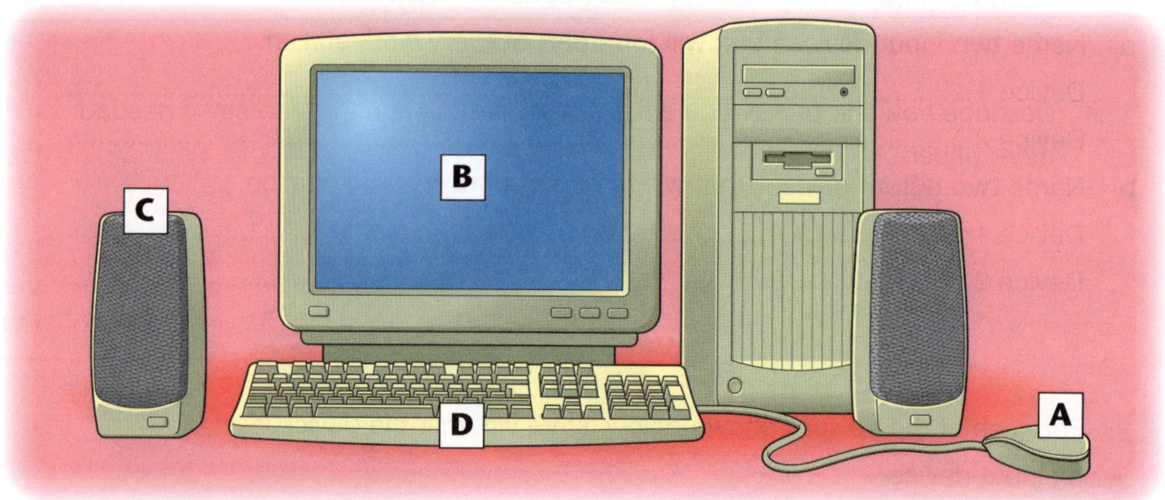

a) Name the parts labelled A, B, C and D.

A .... ①

B .... ①

C .... ①

D .... ①

b) For each part, state if it is an input device or an output device.

A .... ①

B .... ①

C .... ①

D .... ①

TOTAL 8

11 Kieran and Ian use a word processor to do their homework. They were both working at home when there was a power cut. Kieran lost all of his work, but Ian lost only part of his.

a) What had Kieran forgotten to do?

....

.... ②

b) What is auto save?

....

.... ②

c) Explain when you would use **Save** and when you would use **Save As**.

....

....

....

.... ⑥

d) Kieran is waiting for his printer to print 14 pages of his homework. After the third page, a message appears on the screen to say **Printer out of paper**.

   i) ....Where is the message **Printer out of paper** stored?

   .... ①

   ii) Describe how the printer could have signalled the computer to say it needed more paper.

   ....

   .... ②

TOTAL 13

12 A number of everyday objects (other than computers) contain microprocessors. State **three** everyday objects that you would find in your home, which may be controlled by microprocessors.

Object 1 .... ①

Object 2 .... ①

Object 3 .... ①

TOTAL 3

QUESTION BANK ANSWERS

Short-answer questions

① B   ① ② A   ①
③ A   ① ④ D   ①
⑤ B, C, F   ① ⑥ A   ①

Long-answer questions

① a) Hard disk   ①
   b) Any two from: floppy disk; ZIP disk; JAZZ disk; CD-RW or CD-R DVD-RW/DVD-R; magnetic tape.   ②

EXAMINER'S TIP

You will not get marks for a CD-ROM as she cannot update it. She would need a CD-RW, not CD-ROM.

   c) **Controls** the work of the computer system. **Processes** data by performing calculations and decisions. **Stores** data whilst being used.   ③

EXAMINER'S TIP

You will have to use all the correct words to gain marks.

   d) It is temporary so any RAM data that is not saved will be lost.   ②

EXAMINER'S TIP

This is a two-mark question. The examiner is looking for more than a simple statement that RAM is temporary. You must say why this means it is volatile or you will get only one mark.

   e) The operating system displays information to the user in graphical form, e.g. drop-down menus and icons.   ②
   f) Benefit – any one from: no need to remember commands in computer language; can be user-friendly.   ①
      Drawback – any one from: GUIs can be slow to navigate; they need a lot of memory.   ①
   g) Benefits – any one from: relatively cheap to buy; small size; good quality; can print in colour.   ①
      Drawbacks – any one from: relatively slow; expensive to run (cartridges).   ①

② Pen down; forward 50; turn left 90; forward 50; turn left 90; forward 50; turn left 90; forward 50; pen up.   ⑨

EXAMINER'S TIP

You must use the exact instructions given in the table. Do not write anything other than the commands required. You could turn left or right. This type of question gives easy marks as long as you think before you try to answer.

③ Any two of the following: timer; temperature cut out; door sensor to switch on light; temperature setting.   ②

EXAMINER'S TIP

Make sure you do not describe the same device twice using different words. This type of question is aimed at testing your ability to relate what you have learned to a real context. If you think about the question and its relationship to control systems, you should be able to make a good guess at the answer. Put in another practical example if you can.

④ Any of: optical sensor; bumper connected to a micro-switch; sonar.   ①

EXAMINER'S TIP

Make sure you read the question correctly. The type of sensor must be specified.

⑤ a) The infrared beams are broken in a particular sequence which tells the control system whether a car is entering or leaving the car park.   ②
   b) Watch the cars entering or leaving the car park and check that the system is functioning correctly. Check when the car park is empty/full and that the system states that it is empty/full.   ②
   c) Limitation 1: if two cars entered side by side, or too close to each other end to end, they would be counted as only one car.
      Correction 1: redesign the entrance to the car park so that only one car can enter at a time.   ②
      Limitation 2: people could walk past the infrared beams and be counted as a car.
      Correction 2: do not count the number of cars unless both infrared beams are broken at the same time.   ②

EXAMINER'S TIP

Make sure that you do not repeat the same answers, using different words, as you will only receive the marks for an answer once. Use technical terms where they are appropriate.

6 a) A laptop is portable but a PC isn't. **(1)**

b) Laptops can be used in more than one classroom. Laptops can be taken home. No special computer room is needed. **(3)**

c) It's harder to network laptops together. Laptops are more expensive than PCs. Laptops may get damaged more easily than PCs. Laptops may be easier to steal than PCs. **(3)**

7 a) Keyboard and mouse **(2)**

b) Screen and printer **(2)**

8 One mark will be awarded for each correct answer.

Device	Input	Output	Storage
Mouse	x		
Light pen	x		
Printer		x	
Magnetic tape			x
Hard disk			x
Hand-held scanner	x		
Flat screen monitor		x	
Plotter		x	
Digital camera	x		
Zip disk			x

(10)

9 D, F, I, E **(4)**

10 a) A mouse **(1)**
B monitor or VDU **(1)**
C speakers **(1)**
D keyboard **(1)**
b) A input **(1)**
B output **(1)**
C output **(1)**
D input **(1)**

11 a) Kieran had forgotten to save his work at regular intervals. Or he had forgotten to set 'auto save' to save the work automatically. **(2)**

b) Auto Save is a software feature whereby you can tell the software to save the work for you automatically (e.g. every four min). **(2)**

c) The first time you save a new document, you use Save As and the software will ask what name you want to save the document under. Each time you save the document after that, the 'Save' command will overwrite the original document. If you want to retain the original document and also save a new version, you must use the 'Save As' command, and the new version will then have to be given a different name. **(6)**

d) i) It is stored in the computer. **(1)**
ii) It could have achieved this by means of a sensor in the printer which generates a signal that is detected by the computer. **(2)**

12 Answers could include: central heating system; washing machine; watch; dishwasher; handheld calculator; mobile telephone. **(3)**

CHAPTER 2

Inputs, processing and outputs

To revise this topic more thoroughly, see Chapters 1 and 2 in *Letts Revise GCSE Information and Communication Technology Study Guide.*

 Try this sample GCSE question and then compare your answer with the Grade C and Grade A model answers on the pages 22–23.

a　A company is considering the purchase of a camera to add pictures to the company magazine. The company is unsure whether to purchase a conventional 35 mm camera (film based) or a digital camera. Compare the two types of camera, stating the **advantages** and **disadvantages** of each.

[10]

b　The main components of a computer system.

(i)　Use the names below to label the diagram to show the main parts of a computer system.

- monitor
- keyboard
- central processing unit
- CD-ROM
- printer
- disk drive
- mouse

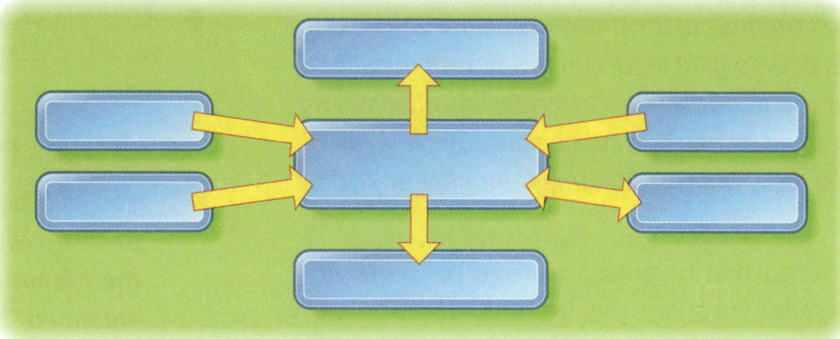

[7]

(ii) State **five** input devices. For **each** input device, give a clear description of its use.

	Device	Description of use
1		
2		
3		
4		
5		

[15]

c The picture below shows three types of concept keyboard.

Describe where a concept keyboard may be used, indicating clearly the reason for its use.

....

....

....

.... [4]

d State **three** output devices and, for each of these, give a clear description of its use.

	Device	Description of use
1		
2		
3		

[9]

e Computers have two sorts of memory: ROM and RAM.

Explain in detail the difference between ROM and RAM memory.

....

....

....

....

....

....

.... [8]

(Total 53 marks)

GRADE C ANSWER

Six marks would be awarded for actually comparing the two cameras in a way the examiner can understand. In this instance, two marks will be awarded as the answer is logically expressed and makes sense, with a total of four additional marks for mentioning: cost; need for film; placing the picture in the magazine; inability to modify the picture using traditional means.

Beth has placed all of the labels in the components, but either did not notice the arrows on the diagram, or guessed the relative positions. Because of this she achieved only three marks out of a possible seven!

Beth has supplied four good input devices but the descriptions are not detailed enough. The fifth input device is actually an output device. This tells the examiner that Beth is not really clear on the names of these devices and how they are used.

Two marks would be awarded: one mark for correct use of concept keyboard; one for stating the reason for its use.

Beth has supplied three good output devices, but the descriptions are very vague. The examiner has awarded one mark for prints out data, because the candidate obviously knows what a printer does, but this is a poor answer. Speakers do not make sounds and the definition for the monitor is also very weak.

Beth has learnt the meaning of the acronyms ROM and RAM, but the definitions, although correct, are very weak. Four marks awarded.

BETH

a Film cameras are cheaper to buy than digital cameras, ✓ but you need to have the film developed ✓ and this would then need to be copied in some way into the company magazine. ✓ You also cannot change the picture in any way. Digital cameras are more expensive but need no film. ✓ The company could put the pictures straight into their magazine, ✓ electronically, and modify pictures ✓ in programs such as Photoshop.

b (i)

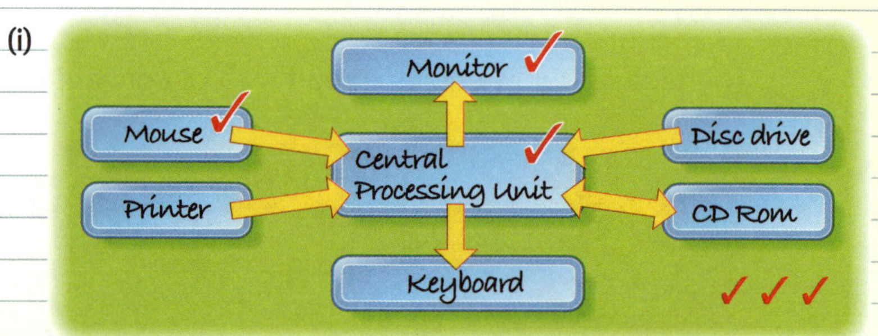

(ii)

	Device	Description of use
1	Keyboard ✓	Used to type text into the computer ✓
2	Mouse ✓	Used to move things around on the screen ✓
3	Joystick ✓	Used in games
4	Light pen ✓	Like mouse but used on the screen ✓
5	Plotter	Plots points on a graph

c Concept keyboards are often used with young children and anywhere that liquid may be spilt. ✓ They are easy to wipe clean. ✓

d

	Device	Description of use
1	Printer ✓	Prints out data ✓
2	Speaker ✓	Makes sounds
3	Monitor ✓	Displays images on screen

e ROM stands for read only memory. ✓ This is memory that the computer can only read information from. ✓ RAM stands for random access memory. ✓ This is memory that the computer can read from and write to. ✓

27 marks = Grade C answer

Grade booster ⟶ move a C to a B

Sometimes questions with a large number of marks are divided into sections. This type of open-ended question is often used towards the end of an exam paper and is used by the examining team to differentiate between Grade C and Grade A candidates. This gives you a good chance to show what you know, both in terms of the question itself and in the use of correct terminology. The number of lines will indicate how much you should write.

Inputs, processing and outputs

GRADE A* ANSWER

Ten marks would be awarded for a very clear comparison, four marks for linking the two options in a very cohesive way, with additional marks for: identifying the need to know whether the magazine is to be produced electronically; mentioning quality of pictures and resolution; mentioning cost; ability to modify digital pictures; ethical issues; mentioning specific applications, e.g. estate agent; use of specialist terminology. To achieve grade A, the answer should be tailored much more closely to the needs of the company as specified in the question.*

Xian has used all of the labels in appropriate parts, showing that he did spot the relevance of the arrows. Seven marks awarded.

Xian has supplied five good devices. The descriptions reflect a knowledge of the use of these devices. Words such as alphanumeric give the examiner a clearer understanding of Xian's knowledge. Xian could probably supply a further four or five input devices with clear and appropriate descriptions of their use.

Four marks would be awarded: one mark for stating two good reasons; one mark for stating place of use; one additional mark for stating why a concept keyboard is more useful than a traditional keyboard; one further mark for stating the advantages in terms of accuracy and speed.

XIAN

a If the company magazine is to be produced electronically, a digital camera has clear advantages over a conventional camera, as the image can be pasted straight into the magazine. ✔✔ To get high quality pictures, the type of digital camera you need is quite expensive compared with the type of resolution ✔ that can be achieved with 35 mm slide film. ✔ The company would need more information on how the magazine is to be compiled and what resolution it is to be compiled in before they could make a final decision. ✔✔ One of the advantages of digital pictures is that they can be easily modified, ✔ or enhanced, ✔ in programs like Photoshop, but if the magazine was, for example, an estate agent's publication, there could be ethical reasons for not wanting this. ✔✔

b (i)

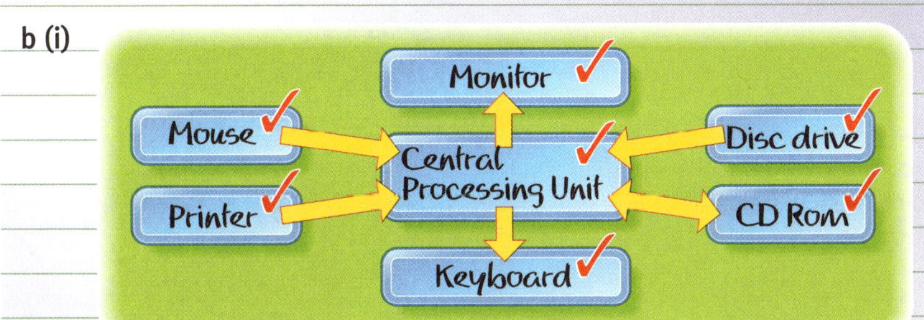

(ii)

	Device	Description of use
1	Keyboard ✔	Used to type in alphanumeric data ✔✔
2	Mouse ✔	Used to control mouse pointer on the screen to access menu commands and other software ✔✔
3	Graphics tablet ✔	Used with a pointer to translate graphic images into a format the computer can draw on the screen ✔✔
4	Digital camera ✔	Used to take photographs which can be converted into digital format to be manipulated on the computer ✔✔
5	Scanner	Works like a photocopier converting each item of information into digital format which can be manipulated on the computer ✔✔

c Concept keyboards are very popular in nurseries for use with young children, as the overlays can be changed. ✔ Concept keyboards are also used in restaurants and bars as they are quick and easy to use and can be easily wiped clean. This makes them hygienic ✔ and more effective ✔ than conventional keyboards in this type of environment. They also avoid typing errors as bar staff simply point and touch the picture of the drink or food item ordered. ✔

Xian has again supplied three good output devices but in this case has also given very clear descriptions of their use, reflecting his knowledge of such devices. The descriptions are in sentences, with technical language used where appropriate.

d

	Device	Description of use
1	Printer ✔	Produces the hard copy of outputs displayed upon the screen, usually on paper but may be on other materials. ✔✔
2	Speaker ✔	Converts digital signals from the computer into sound waves allowing the user to hear output from the computer. ✔✔
3	Monitor ✔	Graphical display unit, allows the user to see what they are working on and interact with the computer in a graphical user interface (G. U. I.) ✔✔

e ROM stands for read only memory. ✔ This is usually the chip or a group of chips in the computer that the main processor can use to control internal devices, ✔ external devices, ✔ and aspects of the software that will not be changed by the user. ✔

RAM stands for random access memory. ✔ This is usually a chip or a group of chips that hold information while the computer is turned on. ✔ This information can be changed by the user, ✔ and when the computer is turned off, the data stored in the RAM is lost. ✔

53 marks = Grade A* answer

Xian has a clear understanding of the words ROM and RAM and what these systems do inside a computer.

Grade booster ····≯ move A to A*

Try to use the correct technical language where possible. Words such as alphanumeric, data, digital, analogue, can help to give the examiner a clearer view of your knowledge. When reading the question, take note of how many marks are to be awarded. Usually one mark is awarded for the name of a device and then two or more marks are awarded for descriptions of its use. If two or more marks are awarded, a sentence should be written.

QUESTION BANK

Short-answer questions

1 The storage device that usually has the largest capacity is:

A a CD-ROM

B a floppy disk

C a ZIP disk

D a DVD. (1)

2 Information on a hard disk is stored:

A magnetically

B using lasers

C in hard copy

D using ink. (1)

3 A laser printer uses:

A ink cartridges

B toner

C correction fluid

D a ribbon. (1)

4 An inkjet printer is:

A an impact printer

B a non-impact printer

C noisy

D expensive to buy compared with other printers. (1)

5 Plotters are available:

A as pen and penless plotters

B only with pens

C only as drum plotters

D only as flatbed plotters. (1)

6 Which storage medium cannot be erased?

A a CD-ROM

B a floppy disk

C magnetic tape storage

D hard disk (1)

7 Indicate which of the following devices are input devices:

A keyboard

B mouse

C printer

D touch screen

E monitor

F digital camera

G scanner

H speaker. (5)

8 Feedback can be described as:

A a computer model

B a loud noise

C an output from a system that is used to influence subsequent input

D an output from a system involving a printer. (1)

9 The process of data capture could involve:

A looking at printed output

B entering, processing and printing results

C collection, verification and input

D collection, entering data and validation. (1)

10 Data can be collected in a computer controlled system using:

A a printer

B multiple choice forms

C a keyboard

D a sensor. (1)

11 A touch-sensitive screen is:

A an input and an output device

B an input device only

C an output device only

D a processing unit. (1)

12 A VDU (visual display unit) is:

A an input and an output device

B an input device only

C an output device only

D a processing unit. (1)

13 Optical character recognition (OCR) refers to:

A a barcode reader

B a device that can read scanned text

C software that can read scanned text

D software that can capture pictures. ①

Long-answer questions

1 Briefly describe the following terms:

- inputs
- storage
- processing
- outputs
- feedback

Inputs ....

.... ②

Storage ....

.... ②

Processing ....

.... ②

Outputs ....

.... ②

Feedback ....

.... ②

TOTAL 10

2 Explain the difference between data and information.

....

....

....

.... ④

TOTAL 4

3

a) State the name given to the keyboards shown in the picture below.

Name .... ①

b) Name three places where this type of keyboard is used. For **each** use, explain
a reason.

....

....

....

....

....

....

⑥

TOTAL 7

4 Standard keyboards have a number of keys including alphabet keys, digit keys
and function keys. What is a function key?

....

....

....

③

TOTAL 3

5 Describe the difference between a tracker ball and a mouse.

....

....

....

③

TOTAL 3

6 Describe the use of the device shown in the picture.

....

....

②

TOTAL 2

7 Two types of scanner are shown in the pictures below. Describe the main differences between them.

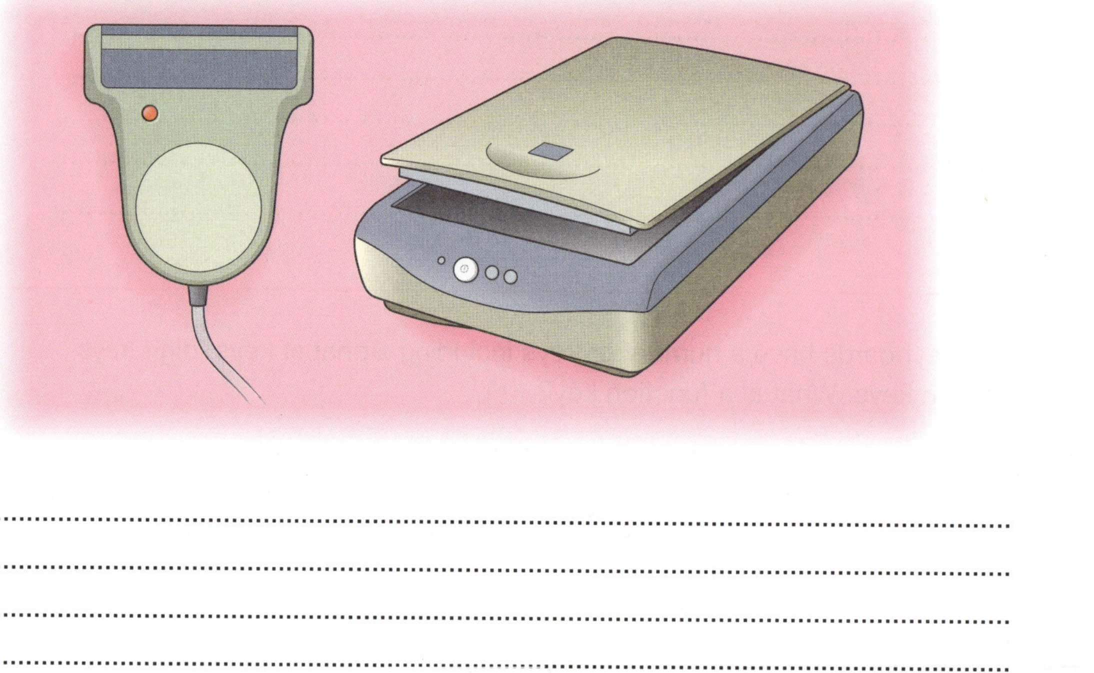

....

....

....

....   ⑤

TOTAL 5

8 The illustration below shows a method of putting data into a system automatically. State the name of the system and give **one** example of its use.

....

....   ②

TOTAL 2

9 The picture below shows a credit card. The credit card contains a magnetic strip. State **one advantage** and **one disadvantage** of using a magnetic strip on a credit card.

Advantage.. ①

Disadvantage .... ①

TOTAL 2

10 Define these terms.

- EPOS
- EFTPOS

EPOS ....

.... ②

EFTPOS ....

.... ②

TOTAL 4

11 The drawings below show three types of computer input device. Name each device.

A .... ①

B .... ①

C .... ①

TOTAL 3

12 Shirley Knott uses a computer-controlled air-conditioning system in her house. She wishes the temperature in the house to be 21 degrees Centigrade.

Explain how Shirley's system will keep the temperature at the right level.

....

....

....

....

....

.... ⑥

TOTAL 6

---

13 Supermarkets sell goods that are marked with bar codes.

a) List **three** pieces of information that are stored in the supermarket computer to enable the bar code system to work.

1.. ①

2.. ①

3.. ①

b) Give **two** reasons why a supermarket would want to use bar codes on food items.

1.. ①

2.. ①

TOTAL 5

---

14 The figure below shows an example of an optical mark sheet. State **two advantages** and **two disadvantages** to a company of using optical mark readers for stock control.

Advantage 1 .... ①

Advantage 2 .... ①

Disadvantage 1.. ①

Disadvantage 2.. ①

TOTAL 4

15 Jonathan Gulley wants to set up an experiment to monitor noise levels on a busy main road. He wishes to conduct the experiment over a two-week period.

a) Name **one** suitable input device he could use.

.... ①

b) Jonathan decides to collect readings once every hour.

   i) What is the data-logging period? .... ①

   ii) What is the data-logging interval? .... ①

c) Explain how Jonathan could use a spreadsheet to analyse the data he collects.

....

....

.... ③

TOTAL 6

---

16 A nuclear power plant has produced a computer model of a nuclear explosion.

a) What is meant by the term 'computer model'?

....

.... ②

b) Explain how a simulation is different to a model.

....

.... ②

c) What are the benefits to the nuclear power plant of using a computer model of a nuclear explosion?

....

.... ②

d) What are the limitations of using a computer model?

....

.... ②

TOTAL 8

---

17 Simon wishes to conduct an experiment into the time it takes boiling water to cool to room temperature.

a) Name a suitable input device he could use to capture the data.

.... ①

b) Suggest a suitable logging interval for the experiment.

.... ①

c) Simon's data-logging device captures the data and saves it in CSV format. Explain why this file format is useful.

....

....

.... ③

TOTAL 5

---

18 When a customer purchases goods from a supermarket, a point of sale system (POS) captures the data.

a) How is data captured by the system?

....

.... ②

b) Where is the price of the item held in the system?

....

.... ②

c) State **two advantages** to the customer of a POS system.

Advantage 1 .... ①

Advantage 2 .... ①

d) State **two advantages** to the supermarket owner of operating a POS system.

Advantage 1 .... ①

Advantage 2 .... ①

TOTAL 8

19 What does the term 'resolution' mean in terms of a computer monitor, and why is it important?

....

....

.... ③

TOTAL 3

20 Three printers are shown below. For each printer, state **one advantage** and **one disadvantage** of using it.

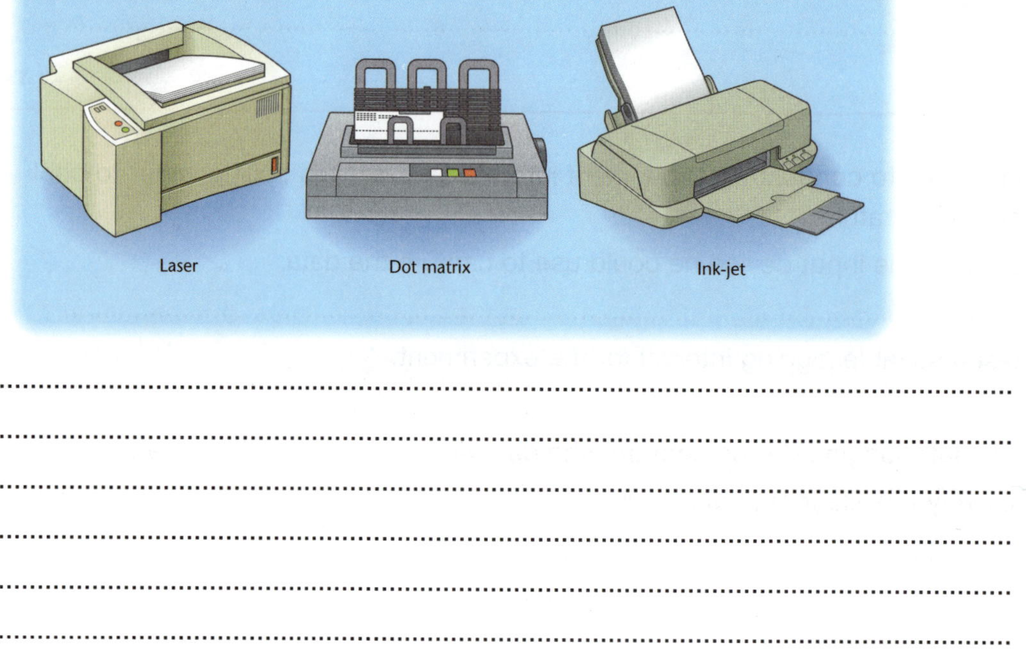

....

....

....

....

....

.... ⑥

TOTAL 6

21 Two ink cartridges are shown below. Explain the difference between them, using examples of their use to clarify your answer.

....

....

....

.... ④

TOTAL 4

22 

a) The picture below shows a flat-bed plotter. State **three** uses of a plotter.

1 .... ①

2 .... ①

3 .... ①

b) Give **one advantage** and **one disadvantage** of using a plotter as opposed to an inkjet printer.

Advantage .... ①

Disadvantage .... ①

TOTAL 5

23 State **two advantages** and **two disadvantages** to a company of using an inkjet printer.

Advantage 1 .... ①
Advantage 2 .... ①
Disadvantage 1 .... ①
Disadvantage 2 .... ①

TOTAL 4

24 State **two advantages** and **two disadvantages** to a company of using a laser printer.

Advantage 1 .... ①
Advantage 2 .... ①
Disadvantage 1 .... ①
Disadvantage 2 .... ①

TOTAL 4

25 State **two advantages** and **two disadvantages** to a company of using a dot matrix printer.

Advantage 1 .... ①
Advantage 2 .... ①
Disadvantage 1 .... ①
Disadvantage 2 .... ①

TOTAL 4

26 State **four** uses of memory in a computer.

Use 1 .... ①
Use 2 .... ①
Use 3 .... ①
Use 4 .... ①

TOTAL 4

27

a) Briefly explain the term **backing store**.

....
.... ②

b) Explain the following terms as they relate to storage media.

Volatility... ①
Storage capacity .... ①
Speed of access... ①
Read capability .... ①
Write capability .... ①

TOTAL 7

28

a) Information is stored in a computer. Name **one** storage medium that has high data storage capacity and can be modified by the user.

....

.... ②

b) Name **one** storage medium that has high capacity but cannot be changed by the user.

.... ①

c) Define the term WORM.

.... ①

d) RAM and ROM are two types of computer memory. Explain the difference between them, giving a working example.

....

....

....

.... ④

TOTAL 8

29 A telephone company currently issues its customers with a paper-based telephone directory of over 2000 pages. It is thinking of making the information available to customers as a CD-ROM.

a) State **one** benefit to customers of using a CD-ROM.

.... ①

b) State **one** benefit to the telephone company of issuing CD-ROMS.

.... ①

c) Explain why not all customers will prefer to have a CD-ROM instead of a paper directory.

....

.... ②

d) Identify **one** other computer-based method of giving telephone numbers to customers.

.... ①

TOTAL 5

Short-answer questions

1. D   (1)
2. A   (1)
3. B   (1)
4. B   (1)
5. A   (1)
6. A   (1)
7. A, B, D, F, G   (5)
8. C   (1)
9. D   (1)
10. D   (1)
11. A   (1)
12. C   (1)

Long-answer questions

1. Inputs are raw data that is fed into a system through input devices such as keyboards and mice. (2)
   Storage can be both temporary and long term and is where data is kept. (2)
   Processing is what the CPU does in a computer when it is calculating, sorting and searching. It turns data into useful information. (2)
   Outputs are the visible or audible results of data processing. They usually appear on a screen or through speakers. (2)
   Feedback is the term used when output from a system is used to influence subsequent input. (2)

EXAMINER'S TIP

When you are asked to describe a term, be brief but precise. Use examples to illustrate your answer where it helps, e.g. for input or output devices.

2. Data is raw values entered into an information system. Information is what you get when data is put into a context that gives it meaning. For example, the sentence 'It is raining today' contains four data items, the words. These are connected together to give information, the sentence. (4)

EXAMINER'S TIP

This answer clearly shows the difference between data and information because it draws upon an everyday example.

3. a) Concept keyboards (1)
   b) In clubs and pubs; for use by young children; anywhere that liquid may be spilled as they can easily be wiped clean. Quick and easy to use so ideal for bars and cinemas; overlays with pictures can be added to make them accessible for young children. (6)

EXAMINER'S TIP

The question specifically asks for reasons why your chosen places use a concept keyboard. Do not simply repeat the same reason for each place or you will gain only one mark.

4. Function keys are numbered F1 to F12 and they control things within a program, such as Help commands. You can usually get extra functions by holding the Shift / Control and Alt keys. Some function keys are controlled by the operating system and enable you to switch the monitor, and other devices, on and off. (3)

EXAMINER'S TIP

The easiest way to answer this question is to give examples of what a function key will do.

5. A tracker ball is like an upside down mouse. You rotate the ball, but the body stays still. Traditional mice use a ball to roll across the table when you move the mouse. (3)

EXAMINER'S TIP

Note that the question asks you to describe the difference, not say what each will do.

6. The picture shows a graphics digitiser or tablet. It is used in design offices to trace technical drawings or produce freehand drawings using computer-aided design software. (2)

EXAMINER'S TIP

Although the question does not ask you to name the device, you will gain extra marks for doing so in your answer.

7. A hand-held scanner is cheaper than a flat-bed scanner, but is more portable. You move the scanner over the picture or source material, whereas the body of a flat-bed scanner does not move. You place the source material on the glass plate. (5)

EXAMINER'S TIP

Note that the question asks you to describe the difference, not say what each will do.

8 Optical mark recognition form, used in surveys and exam papers. **2**

EXAMINER'S TIP

9 It makes the card easy and quick to use; the strip cannot hold much data; it can be damaged by a strong magnet; it is cheap to produce; reading magnetic strips is accurate and fast. **2**

EXAMINER'S TIP

Although the question asks for one advantage and one disadvantage, it is worth putting down all of the points you can think of if you have time.

10 EPOS stands for electronic point of sale; is commonly found in shops, where it uses bar code readers, touch screens and keyboards to capture sales information and produce itemised bills.
EFTPOS stands for electronic funds transfer at point of sale; is also commonly found in shops, where it enables the shop to take funds direct from a customer's bank account, providing a much faster method of payment than cheques or cash. **2**

EXAMINER'S TIP

Always try to give examples of use as this will help you gain maximum marks and show the examiner that you really know what you are talking about.

11 A Scanner **1**
B Stylus or light pen **1**
C Joystick **1**

EXAMINER'S TIP

A clue is given in the question, as you know they are all input devices. If you are not quite sure what one of the drawings represents, guess an answer – remembering that they are all computer input devices.

12 Any six from the following list. A thermostat is set to 21 degrees Centigrade. The thermostat measures the temperature inside the house. Data from the thermostat is analysed by a processor. The processor compares the current temperature with the target temperature. If the temperature is below the target level, a signal is sent to switch on a heater. If the temperature is above the target level, a signal is sent to switch on a cooler. If the temperature is at the correct level, both the heater and the cooler are switched off. The system uses feedback. **6**

EXAMINER'S TIP

To help you, examiners often highlight key words in the question. Look for these before answering a question. Some candidates find it useful to read through the question and pick out the key words for themselves with a highlighter pen.

13 a) Any three of the following: price, quantity in stock, item description, item and bar code number, supplier, manufacturer. **3**

EXAMINER'S TIP

Do not simply repeat the same answer, e.g. item number, shop number. Always try to give three different pieces of information as you can only gain marks once for any given answer.

b) Any two of the following: processing at the tills is faster, there are fewer errors, stock control is automatic, there is less manual keying in, validation is easy. **2**

EXAMINER'S TIP

These answers follow on from the previous question. Think about your answers there and the benefits to the supermarket.

14 Advantages – OMR readers are much quicker than keyboards as you do not have to type things in; OMR readers can process very large amounts of data very quickly. **2**
Disadvantages – OMR forms must be completed very accurately, or the reader will not be able to read the marks; any damage to the OMR sheet, such as creasing, folding or dirt, can be read by the reader as a mark. **2**

15 a) Noise sensor microphone **1**

b) i) Two weeks **1**

EXAMINER'S TIP

You have to look for the answer to this in the question. Do not just guess.

ii) One hour **1**

EXAMINER'S TIP

Again, the answer to this is in the question. Do not just guess.

c) The data could be entered with the time as one column and the reading as another column. He could use formulae to calculate information such as the average noise level. He could display the results in a chart or graph. **3**

16 a) A model is a set of equations and instructions designed to represent a real-world event. **2**

b) A simulation is the output of running a model. **2**

c) Less expensive than a real explosion. The model can be run many times. **2**

d) The model may not be completely accurate. This means that the simulation may produce inaccurate results. **2**

17 a) Temperature sensor, thermistor **1**

EXAMINER'S TIP

You will not get marks for a thermometer.

b) Anything suitable, e.g. once a minute, twice a minute etc. **1**

c) CSV stands for comma-separated-variable, where each item of data is separated by a comma. It means that the data can be imported directly into a table or spreadsheet. **3**

18 a) A bar code is scanned. **2**

EXAMINER'S TIP

Two marks are possible so the answer must be more than one word.

b) Each item will be a record in a computer file in the main computer. **2**

EXAMINER'S TIP

Remember that a shop will use a mainframe computer and the tills are simply terminals.

c) Any two from the following list. It will be faster through the checkout, which will lead to shorter queues. There will be fewer mistakes and better stock control, which should prevent the shop from running out of items. It will give the customer a fully itemised shopping bill. **2**

d) Any two from the following list. There is no need to pay staff to put price labels on every item. The manager will be able to monitor the performance of individual checkout staff. Fewer checkout staff will be required. There is less chance of an error at the checkout. Stock control is automatic. **2**

EXAMINER'S TIP

Even if there are similar benefits to both manager and customers, do not list the same benefit twice. Examiners are looking for different answers for each part. This type of question can usually be answered from general knowledge of POS systems. Imagine the differences between the shops of today and shops before computerisation, and guess the answers if you are not sure of a response.

19 Resolution relates to the separate units of light, also known as pixels, shown on a screen. It is important because, the higher the resolution, the clearer the screen image will be. **3**

EXAMINER'S TIP

Make sure you relate your answer to a computer monitor and not to a printout or photograph.

20 **Dot matrix printer** – noisy and low quality printout but can be used with multi-part stationery. It is cheap to buy compared with other printers. Uses ribbons which are cheap compared with ink cartridges and toner cartridges. **2**

Laser printer – high quality printouts, and fast, but expensive compared with other printers. Toner refills are quite expensive but produce a large number of copies. **2**

Inkjet printer – high quality printing at fairly low cost, but needs special paper and is slower than a laser printer. You need to buy ink cartridges. Inkjet printers take up less desk space than laser printers, and are almost silent in use. **2**

EXAMINER'S TIP

If you are going to say something is cheap, you must clarify your answer by stating what it is cheaper than. You will not get marks just by saying cheap.

21 Normal ink jet printers use three-colour cartridges, plus black. Photo quality inkjet printers use five colours, plus black. This gives a much better quality image, where photo quality is needed. If normal printing is the main use of the printer, it is better to use a three-colour cartridge as these are cheaper to buy and contain more ink in standard colours. **4**

EXAMINER'S TIP

For this question you must explain why some inkjet printers have five-colour cartridges to get maximum marks. You should make it clear why someone would want each type of printer.

22 a) To produce plans, maps, line diagrams, three-dimensional drawings, electronic circuit diagrams. **3**

b) Plotters are slower, but far more accurate. They can work on much larger paper. Design drawings and technical drawings would be produced on a plotter as accuracy, and not speed of output, is needed. **2**

EXAMINER'S TIP

The use of an example helps the candidate to gain maximum marks for this question.

23 Advantage – not too expensive to buy; silent to operate; usually takes up less space on the desk. **2**
Disadvantage – needs special paper; running cost quite high. **2**

24 Advantage – fast in operation; high quality output; print on normal paper. **2**
Disadvantage – expensive to buy; toner cartridges are expensive to buy; printer usually takes up quite a lot of desktop. **2**

25 Advantage – you can use multi-part stationery; print on normal paper; cheap to buy; low cost ribbon. **2**
Disadvantage – noisy in operation; low quality output. **2**

26 To hold programs, to hold data that has been input, to provide a working area to store data that is being processed, to hold data that is bound for an output device. **4**

EXAMINER'S TIP

Be careful with this type of question because it is easy to repeat yourself. For example, stating that memory holds programs and holds the operating system. The operating system is, of course, a program, so you would gain only one mark for these two points.

27 a) The backing store holds data outside the central processing unit, in some kind of storage medium. **2**

b) Volatility – will the data be lost when power is removed? **1**
Storage capacity – how much data can the medium hold? **1**
Speed of access – how fast can the medium be read or written to? **1**

Read capability – how easy is it to read the data on the medium and what special hardware/software is needed? **1**
Write capability– how easy is it to write data to the medium and what special hardware/software is needed? **1**

28 a) Any one of the following: hard disk/magnetic optical disk/tape D drive/read-write optical disk/ ZIP and ZAP disk. **2**

b) CD-ROM **1**

c) Write Once Read Many Times **1**

EXAMINER'S TIP

Each question is worth a single mark, but you must use the correct terminology, so in b) CD would not gain a mark. CD-ROM is the correct computing term.

d) RAM is volatile; ROM is non-volatile. The user can change RAM contents but cannot change ROM contents. ROM is used to hold the operating system/BIOS. RAM is used to hold the user's programs and data. **4**

EXAMINER'S TIP

The last part of questions is usually the hardest, particularly on Higher tier papers. This question contains four parts: what is ROM, what is RAM, and for each give an example. It is very easy to miss out part of the answer and lose valuable marks.

29 a) CD-ROM is smaller/lighter than a paper directory. **1**

b) Cheaper to send to customers than paper directories. **1**

c) Any two from the following list. Some customers do not have a computer. Some customers will find it quicker to obtain numbers from the paper directory. Paper directory can be kept by the telephone. Paper directory more portable. **2**

d) Internet, DVD. **1**

EXAMINER'S TIP

No marks for floppy disk as these have insufficient memory.

Operating environments

To revise this topic more thoroughly, see Chapter 3 in *Letts Revise GCSE Information and Communication Technology Study Guide*.

Try this sample GCSE question and then compare your answer with the Grade C and Grade A model answers on pages 41 and 42.

a   The operating system of modern computers has progressed from a command-driven system to a graphical user interface (GUI).

Describe **three** advantages to the user of using a graphical user interface rather than a command-driven system.

1..

.... **[2]**

2..

.... **[2]**

3..

.... **[2]**

b   'The operating system is the software heart of the machine.' In the space below, give a detailed explanation of what the operating system of a modern PC does.

....

....

....

....

....

....

....

....

....

....

.... **[12]**

(Total 18 marks)

 These two answers are at grades C and A. Compare which one your answer is closest to and think how you could have improved it.

GRADE C ANSWER

These answers reflect some understanding of the term 'graphical user interface'. However, Rose has not been able to give very detailed descriptions. Four marks total.

Rose seems to know what an operating system is, but it can be very difficult to supply a good answer. The candidate starts off well but then falls into the trap of listing different versions of operating systems. Although this shows some background knowledge, it is not relevant to the answer. One mark is awarded for knowing that different computer systems may use different operating systems. Seven marks awarded.

ROSE

a 1 The user does not have to type in commands. You just move a mouse around the screen, pointing at icons. ✓

2 The user can have different colours on the screen to make it easier to read text or view images. ✓✓

3 The user can have pictures on the desktop, making the screen more personal. ✓

b The operating system controls all the elements of the computer ✓ allowing different software applications to communicate between each other ✓ and to communicate with the hardware contained within the box. ✓ An operating system such as Windows ✓ allows the user to communicate with different aspects of the machine ✓ as well as allowing the computer to communicate with the user. ✓ There are a number of different operating systems, Windows 98, Windows 2000, Windows NT, Windows Millennium, Windows X.P. On Apple Macs, a different operating system, called OS 10, is used. ✓

11 marks = Grade C answer

Grade booster ⸱⸱⸱⟩ move a C to a B

Do not just list software; try to make valid general points and think about the end user. Don't waffle just to fill the space. The examiner will see through this and give fewer, not more, marks.

GRADE A ANSWER

These answers carry a lot more detail. Amale has been able to show her understanding of the difference between the GUI and a command system, using examples where appropriate. The examiner can clearly see that Amale knows what she is talking about, even though this answer is a little confusing, and not strictly correct. Five marks awarded.

Amale has a clearer understanding of what an operating system does. She is also able to communicate this to the examiner, making good, valid and justified points.

AMALE

a 1 A GUI allows more information to be conveyed to the user through the use of icons, pictures, text and moving images. ✓✓

2 Icons can make it easier for a user to know what a computer is going to do before it does it. If you want to load Word, for example, you click on the icon that has a W on it. ✓

3 Using a mouse is a lot quicker than typing in commands. It allows the user to carry out much more complex operations in a much easier way. For instance, opening a file that has been saved before can be done by clicking on a folder and then clicking on the filename. With a command system, you would have to know the filename and the directory structure, to be able to find a file and then open it. ✓✓

b An operating system allows the user to use an interface ✓ that makes carrying out tasks on a personal computer easier ✓ and much more efficient. ✓ On all operating systems there is a button that you can click to get at everything you need. This button can start programs, open documents and change the computer settings. ✓ Modern PCs have a desktop. ✓ This also makes it easier to start tasks and find connections to other resources in the computer, both software and hardware. ✓ The user can just point and click. ✓ The operating system allocates memory ✓ and other resources to each piece of software or hardware running on the machine. ✓ It also runs the clock which keeps everything running together. ✓ It also allows all the different bits to communicate ✓ by translating information from the user, software, hardware and other devices. ✓

17 marks = Grade A answer

Grade booster ⋯⟩ move A to A*

To get full marks, look at how many marks are available and make sure you include at least this many points in your answer.

Short-answer questions

1 A record in a database has a structure. Does the structure define:

A the size of the file

B the name, length and type of field

C the length of the record

D how many records are in a file. ①

2 A computer model is used to:

A describe an object

B create an animation

C design computer programs

D simulate real events. ①

3 A computer simulation can be described as:

A a computer model

B slowed down animation

C a robot controlled by a computer

D the output of a computer model. ①

4 Systems software:

A can be described as spreadsheets, word processing and databases

B controls the computer operating system

C exists only in solid state

D uses a graphical user interface. ①

5 Applications software:

A can be described as spreadsheets, word processing and databases

B controls the computer operating system

C exists only in solid state

D uses a graphical user interface. ①

6 When a computer is multi-tasking, it is:

A running one program at a time

B performing calculations in a spreadsheet

C running two or more programs at a time

D printing out a document. ①

7 Which of the following can be described as a system utility?

A a database

B a defragmentation program

C a calculator

D a spreadsheet ①

Long-answer questions

1

a) Define the term '**operating environment**'.

....
.... ②

b) Define the term '**user interface**', giving examples.

....
....
....
....
....
....
....
.... ⑧

TOTAL 10

2 Give **three** typical functions of an operating system.

Function 1...

.... ②

Function 2...

.... ②

Function 3...

.... ②

TOTAL 6

3 Describe the differences between a high level and a low level programming language.

....

....

....

.... ④

TOTAL 4

4 George Barker has recently installed a new operating system on his computer.

a) Describe the main functions of an operating system.

....

....

.... ③

b) Identify **two** utility programs used by an operating system.

Program 1 .... ①

Program 2 .... ①

c) The operating system uses a command-driven user interface.

   i) What does command-driven user interface mean?

.... ①

   ii) Give **one** benefit and **one** drawback of a command-driven user interface.

Benefit .... ①

Drawback.. ①

TOTAL 8

5 Melanie Driver is the network manager of a large secondary school. Every week she runs a back-up of all the data stored on the network. Melanie uses the ancestral method.

What is the ancestral method of file back-up?

....

....

.... ③

TOTAL 3

Short-answer questions

1. B — 1
2. D — 1
3. D — 1
4. B — 1
5. A — 1
6. C — 1
7. B — 1

Long-answer questions

1. a) Operating environment refers to the interaction of an information system, typically a computer system, with the user. — 2

   b) The user interface, also known as human computer interface (HCI), is the means of communication between the computer user and the system. The interface usually uses cursors, prompts, icons and menus. It can be command driven, where the user has to enter a command, usually using a keyboard. It can be menu driven, where the user chooses a list of commands using a mouse, touch screen or keyboard. It can be graphical, often called GUI (graphical user interface), where commands are given using menus and pointers. — 8

2. Allocating a time slot for each job that the processor needs to undertake; allocating memory for programs and data; ensuring that different jobs are prioritised in the correct order; controlling data storage and keeping track of the space available; controlling the routines for input and output operations; accepting commands and data from the user via the input devices; interpretation of commands; transfer of data to memory; management of system security. — 6

3. Low level means that a programming language is easy for the computer to understand, although it is more difficult for the programmer to understand. High level programming languages have been developed to make it easier to program. They are often written in a form not too different from everyday language. — 4

4. a) Any three from: monitors the performance of the system; enables software to communicate with hardware (e.g. entering text on a keyboard); enables applications software to be loaded; gives prompts and error reports to the user; allocates processor time to various tasks. — 3

   b) Virus scanning software; print managers. — 2

   c) i) The user gives instructions by **typing commands** onto the computer. — 1

      ii) One from the following list. Benefit: commands can be given more quickly than using a menu-driven system; takes up less memory than a menu-driven system. Drawback: the user needs to know the computer language needed to give instructions. — 2

5. Three from the following list. Three back-up copies are kept. The most recent copy is called the son. When the next backup is made the son becomes the father copy and the new copy is the son. When the next backup is made the father becomes the grandfather (oldest) copy. When the next backup is made the grandfather copy is erased. — 3

CHAPTER 4

Applications software

To revise this topic more thoroughly, see Chapter 3 in *Letts Revise GCSE Information and Communication Technology Study Guide*.

 Try this sample GCSE question and then compare your answer with the Grade C and Grade A model answers on pages 47 and 48.

a Different software applications are used to carry out different tasks. The following users have each decided to purchase software for their computer. For each, state the type of application they would find useful and explain why they should purchase it.

Graphic designer
Retired person
Teenager
Author
Accountant
Stock controller

[12]

b Describe **three** advantages to an employer of installing a computer system to calculate the wages for the staff and state **two** different disadvantages that the staff may suffer following the introduction of the computer system to calculate the wages.

....

....

....

....

....

....

....

....

....

.... [10]

(Total 22 marks)

GRADE C ANSWER

Dave has failed to explain any of the recommendations, immediately losing six marks. He has also fallen into the trap of naming software titles, rather than the type. The accountant may well use a spreadsheet, but not necessarily Excel. E-mail is a system, not a software application. An MP3 player is a device, not a software application. Three marks awarded.

Dave has written three simple advantages, the third of which does not justify the awarding of a mark. The first two, however, are worth one mark each, from a potential two each. Dave has then gone on to repeat the first descriptions as disadvantages, ignoring the question instruction calling for different descriptions. He has not shown an understanding of the implications of the installation of the new equipment, and has therefore not achieved a high mark. Two marks awarded.

DAVE

a	Graphic designer	Photo editing software ✓
	Retired person	E-mail
	Teenager	Mp3 player
	Author	Word processor ✓
	Accountant	Excel
b	Stock controller	Database ✓

The employer will get accurate figures for the wages, ✓ the employer will be able to sack the people who do the wages now. ✓ The employer will be able to use the computer for other things. ✓ The staff may be sacked and they will not be able to fiddle the wages because the computer is more accurate. ✓

5 marks = Grade C answer

Applications software

Barbara has correctly identified appropriate software and given a clear explanation of why the software would be useful. She has given more than one example in some cases and this shows the examiner that she knows about a range of software, not just the main office applications. Twelve marks awarded.

BARBARA

a

Graphic designer	Photo editing and scanning software, linked to a desktop publishing application, ✓ to allow the designer to scan in images, edit them and then publish them ✓
Retired person	A general office system, with word processing, e-mail and database software, ✓ so that they can type letters, store addresses and e-mail their friends and relations ✓
Teenager	Games and music software ✓ so that they can use the computer as an entertainment centre ✓
Author	A word processor, ✓ so that they can type books ✓
Accountant	Spreadsheets and databases, ✓ so that they can do their calculations and store their clients' information ✓
Stock controller	Database ✓ to store the details of incoming and outgoing stock ✓

Barbara has laid the answer out well, clearly breaking it into parts. Each part gives a clear advantage or disadvantage with an elaborated response, showing their understanding of the subject matter. Eight marks awarded.

b Three advantages for installing a computer for the wages are:

1 The calculations will be accurate and can be altered quickly if someone does some overtime. ✓

2 The calculations will be done quicker, so wages will be given out on time. ✓

3 The employer can get rid of the wages staff, saving money on wages. ✓✓

Two disadvantages for the staff are:

1 The staff will lose the face to face contact with the person who works out the wages. ✓✓

2 The staff will feel that they may lose their jobs because of the introduction of computers. ✓✓

20 marks = Grade A answer

Short-answer questions

1 A shopkeeper stores details of stock on a computer. The software he/she uses is called:

A a word-processing package

B a database package

C a spreadsheet package

D a graphics package. ①

2 A database contains a gender field. Which of the following would be the most likely coding for this field?

A female / male

B f / m

C sex 1 / sex 2

D 1 / 2 ①

3 Spreadsheets are used by shops to keep an ongoing record of sales. The most important feature of the spreadsheet model is:

A the fonts used

B fill down and replication options

C formulae in cells

D the colour of numbers in cells. ①

4 Which of the following is an example of an applications package?

A a user guide

B a CD-ROM driver

C an operating system

D a payroll and taxation program ①

5 A word processor is used for:

A analysing figures

B creating, formatting and editing documents

C storing information

D storing information on people. ①

6 What basic tools would you find in the Edit menu of a word processor?

A clear, replace and header

B spelling, grammar and auto correct

C cut, copy, replace, paste and clear

D language and track changes ①

7 What is a header?

A text at the bottom of every page

B numbers which appear on every page

C text that appears at the top of every page

D text in the centre of every page ①

8 A spreadsheet is used to:

A analyse data

B write letters

C create music

D draw pictures. ①

9 A database is used to:

A analyse and manipulate numerical information

B produce high quality documents

C organise, store and sort information

D design page layouts. ①

10 A database record contains:

A numbers

B information about certain programs

C all the data about one specific item

D text. ①

11 A database report is:

A a way of extracting information from the database

B a very flexible way of creating and editing documents

C a link between databases over the internet

D a method of calculating the number of records in other databases. ①

Long-answer questions

1 Ivy Cutter has used a word-processor to write a piece of GCSE coursework.

Explain how each of the following functions has helped her:

a) Spell-check facility

....

.... ②

b) Header

....

.... ②

c) Word-count.

.... ①

TOTAL 5

2 Gina Rhodes has been asked to produce her school's newsletter. She wishes to include a number of photographs in the newsletter. Some have been taken with a digital camera, others are prints taken using a film camera.

a) Which applications software would be most suitable for producing the newsletter?

.... ①

b) Describe **two** features of this software that would make it suitable for the task.

Feature 1... ①

Feature 2... ①

c) Explain how Gina could put the photographic prints into her newsletter.

....

....

.... ③

TOTAL 6

3 Mike Stodgley is a member of a fishing club. He wants to produce a monthly newsletter. Explain how he could use publishing software to produce the newsletter.

....

....

....

....

....

....

.... ⑦

TOTAL 7

4 Four types of justification are shown below. Label each illustration to show the type of justification used.

A	B	C	D
This text is justified how is it justified? This text is justified how? This text is justified how is it justified? This text is justified how? This text is justified how is it justified? This text is justified	This text is justified how is it justified? This text is justified how? This text is justified how is it justified? This text is justified how? This text is justified how is it justified? This text is justified	This text is justified how is it justified? This text is justified how? This text is justified how is it justified? This text is justified how? This text is justified how is it justified? This text is justified	This text is justified how is it justified? This text is justified how? This text is justified how is it justified? This text is justified how? This text is justified how is it justified? This text is justified

A .... ①

B .... ①

C .... ①

D .... ①

TOTAL 4

5 A school office uses computerised word processing. Explain three ways word processing could be used to help with the school administration.

Way 1 .... ①

Way 2 .... ①

Way 3 .... ①

TOTAL 3

6 Describe what is meant by **mail merge**, giving **one** example of its use.

....

....

....

.... ④

TOTAL 4

7 Chloe often uses a word processor to write to her friends. Every time she carries out a spell check, the word processor tells her that her best friend's name is mis-spelt. She knows that it is spelt correctly.

a) Describe how Chloe could avoid this message appearing.

.... ①

b) Chloe gets the same message each time she enters a postcode. State what action Chloe should take.

.... ①

c) Why would the action Chloe takes with regard to her friend's name differ from the action she would take with the postcode?

....

.... ②

d) It takes Chloe a long time to type in her friends' addresses. How can Chloe make it easier to set up a page ready for future letters to her friends?

....

....

.... ③

TOTAL 7

8 Two letters are shown below.

a) State **four** changes that have been made to the second letter and, for each change, describe the word-processing software feature that has been used.

Change 1 .... ①

Feature used... ①

Change 2 .... ①

Feature used... ①

Change 3 .... ①

Feature used... ①

Change 4 .... ①

Feature used... ①

<table>
<tr><td>

16, Springfield Close,
Warrington,
Durham.

19th July 2002

Dear <title> <surname>,

With reference to your recent letter relating to account <account>, we regret to inform you that the outstanding balance of <balance> has been refused by your bank.

Please pay the outstanding amount as soon as possible. Any delay will result in additional interest charges.

We look forward to hearing from you soon.

Yours sincerely

Joe Soap, Accounts

</td><td>

16, Springfield Close,
Warrington,
Durham.

19th July 2002

Dear <title> <surname>,

With reference to your recent letter relating to account <account>, we regret to inform you that the outstanding balance of <balance> has been refused by your bank.

Please pay the outstanding amount as soon as possible. Any delay will result in additional interest charges.

We look forward to hearing from you soon.

Yours sincerely

Joe Soap, Accounts

</td></tr>
</table>

b) Underline the places in the letter that have been set up to enable the company to use a mail merge facility.

> 16, Springfield Close,
> Warrington,
> Durham.
>
> **19th July 2002**
>
> Dear <title> <surname>,
>
> With reference to your recent letter relating to account <account>, we regret to inform you that the outstanding balance of <balance> has been refused by your bank.
>
> Please pay the outstanding amount as soon as possible. Any delay will result in additional interest charges.
>
> We look forward to hearing from you soon.
>
> Yours sincerely
>
> Joe Soap, Accounts

④

c) What other piece of information in the letter should be inside mail merge markers to enable the company to use the mail merge facility?

.... ①

TOTAL 13

---

9 Discuss the **advantages** and **disadvantages** of using word-processed text together with electronic mail, as opposed to a paper-based system to send letters.

....
....
....
....
....
.... ⑥

TOTAL 6

---

10 Mavis Deacon stores details of her customers on a computer database. One of the **fields** is called TOWN.

a) Explain the difference between a **field** and a **record**.

....
.... ②

b) How could Mavis produce a list of all the customers who live in the town of Alice Springs?

....
.... ②

TOTAL 4

11 Gina Spright has collected data on how much each member of her class spends on magazines each month. She wishes to display this information in a graph.

a) Name **one** suitable graph that Gina could use.

.... ①

b) Explain how Gina could use her computer to produce the graph.

....

....

....

.... ④

c) Gina wishes to send a copy of the graph to her friend in Australia. Describe how Gina could use e-mail to do this.

....

....

....

.... ④

TOTAL 9

12 Hillview Holiday Cottages stores information about its customers on its computer system. The business wishes to send a personalised letter to all its customers who live in the town of Halmorden.

a) Which applications software is the business likely to use to store the customer information?

.... ①

b) Explain how the business could produce the list of customers.

....

.... ②

c) Explain how the business could use mail merge to produce the letters.

....

....

....

.... ④

TOTAL 7

13 Jane Smiley uses a spreadsheet to record information about the results of her pupils in an examination. Part of the spreadsheet is shown below.

	A	B	C	D
1	Name	Mark out of 40	Percentage	Pass or Fail
2	Mark Wisely	32	80	PASS
3	Phil Down	20		
4	Sue Anyone	16		
5	Cal Kewlator	34		
6	Fred Needle	40		
7	Doug Knightly	23		
8	Penny Markup	6		
9				
10	Average			

a) Which formula has been entered into cell C2?

.... ①

b) Which spreadsheet function would save time when entering the other formulae in column C?

.... ①

c) The pass mark is 50%. Explain how the data in cell D2 has been produced by the computer.

....

.... ②

d) Jane wishes to adapt the spreadsheet so that she can easily see which pupil has scored the highest mark in the test. Name **one** method she could use to do this.

.... ①

TOTAL 5

14 When a user searches a database, he or she sets up a search condition, often called a query. For example, if the user wants to find all of the boys with birthdays on 15th February, he or she would carry out a search condition to find the people with the right birthday and the correct sex. The table on the next page shows one screen of a database.

Family name	Given name	Sex	Date of birth	Address	Doctor
Asham	Mayer	M	10-12-75	22, High Street	Smith
Cushing	Xian	M	11-9-74	45, Main Road	Smith
Davidson	Jim	M	15-2-76	21, The Slade	Johns
Inskip	Donald	M	2-6-73	12, The Slade	Smith
Morey	Lesley	F	23-6-74	6, Ash Row	Johns
Price	Jill	F	29-9-73	The Mill, High Street	Smith
Yates	Barbara	F	31-2-75	12, Flower Pot Road	Johns

a) State which field has been used to sort the data, and how the data has been sorted.

.... ①

b) There is a data entry error in the date field, where one of the dates of birth is incorrect. Which date of birth is incorrect?

.... ①

c) Describe how the database could have been set up to avoid this data entry error.

.... ①

d) Describe how you could search for all males born after 1994.

....

.... ②

e) What is a field length?

....

.... ②

f) What is a true/false field?

....

.... ②

TOTAL 9

15 There are a number of different types of databases. For each of the following, describe what type of database the term refers to.

a) A distributed database

....

....

.... ③

b) A relational database

....

....

.... ③

TOTAL 6

(16) A school shop uses a spreadsheet to monitor the sale of text books to children. Part of the spreadsheet is shown below.

	A	B	C	D
1	Description	Selling price £	Number sold	Sales value
2	ICT textbook	11.75	104	1222.00
3	Food textbook	12.50	94	1175.00
4	Maths textbook	14.00	180	2520.00
5	English textbook	10.75	190	2042.50
6	Science textbook	16.50	130	2145.00
7	Total sales		698	9104.50
8				

a) Write down the formula that would be entered into the shaded cells.

	A	B	C	D
1	Description	Selling price £	Number sold	Sales value
2	ICT textbook	11.75	104	1222.00
3	Food textbook	12.50	94	1175.00
4	Maths textbook	14.00	180	2520.00
5	English textbook	10.75	190	2042.50
6	Science textbook	16.50	130	2145.00
7	Total sales		698	9104.50
8				

③

b) Write down **two** advantages to the shop of using formulae in a spreadsheet.

Advantage 1 .... ①

Advantage 2 .... ①

c) The school shop modifies the spreadsheet in order to calculate profits from sales.

	A	B	C	D	E	F
1	Description	Selling price £	Number sold	Sales value	Purchase price	Profit on sales
2	ICT textbook	11.75	104	1222.00	10.00	182.00
3	Food textbook	12.50	94	1175.00	10.25	211.50
4	Maths textbook	14.00	180	2520.00	12.50	270.00
5	English textbook	10.75	190	2042.50	9.25	285.00
6	Science textbook	16.50	130	2145.00	14.00	325.00
7	Total sales		698	9104.50		1273.50
8						

Show the formula that has been added to the shaded cell.

.... ①

d) The profit shown in F7 is to be added to another spreadsheet used by the school to indicate the school's present financial position. The data is to be updated automatically. Describe how this could be achieved.

....

.... ②

TOTAL 8

17 A local restaurant's spreadsheet used to model profits is shown below. To calculate the column headed hours, the restaurant has divided the total number of one-off items made into the total time it took the chef to make the batch of items. The ingredient costs have been calculated by dividing total purchase price of the ingredients by the number of food items that can be produced from the ingredients bought. The restaurant uses two chefs. The pastry chef is paid at a higher rate than the general chef.

	A	B	C	D	E	F
1	Menu costing sheet					
2	Lunchtime set menu					
3	Description	Hours	Labour cost / hour	Ingredients cost	Overheads	Cost
4	Vegetable soup	0.25	5.60	0.50	0.20	
5	Salad	0.30	5.60	1.50	0.10	
6	Bread roll	0.10	6.50	0.10	0.12	
7	Butter	0.00	0.00	0.08	0.11	
8	Apple pie	0.30	6.50	1.25	0.30	
9						
10						

a) Write down the formula that would be entered in cell F4 to calculate the total cost of the vegetable soup.

....

.... ②

b) State how you would set up a formula in the other cells under column F.

.... ①

c) What formula would the restaurant use to calculate the total cost of the meal?

....

.... ②

d) The pastry chef has asked for a pay rise. The restaurant does not want to put up its prices. Explain how the restaurant could use a computer model to explore changes in profit margins in order to establish the effects of increasing the pay of the pastry chef.

....

....

....

.... ④

TOTAL 9

18 A school uses a spreadsheet to keep track of student payments towards a skiing holiday in France. The spreadsheet will show payments and costs related to transport and hotels. Describe the main features of a spreadsheet that would allow a teacher to find the best possible prices for hotel booking and transport.

....

....

....

....

.... ⑤

TOTAL 5

19 Your school has decided to introduce a computerised system for checking the attendance of pupils. Each pupil is issued with a SMART card. The SMART card is scanned via readers in each classroom. Describe the main stages that would need to be undertaken before the system can be operational.

....

....

....

....

.... ⑤

TOTAL 5

20 Compare a range of methods of obtaining pictures or graphics for inclusion in a desktop publishing package.

....

....

....

....

....

....

.... ⑦

TOTAL 7

21 The following chart shows a shop's database.

Customer reference	Family name	First name	Gender	Address one	Address two
45896	Patel	Sanjit	m	12, Corn Street	Towcester
98356	Vindis	Kurt	m	37, Main Road	Bungay
12580	Allday	Sonia	f	163, Walnut Close	Bedford

a) How many records are shown?

.... ①

b) How many fields are shown?

.... ①

c) Name four other column headings that could be included.

1... ①
2... ①
3... ①
4... ①

TOTAL 6

22 The chart below shows a company database held in a spreadsheet.

1	Family name	Hours worked	Pay per hour	Gross pay
2	Whitemarsh	12	4.50	
3	Sole	36	6.75	
4	Raymond	25	4.50	
5	Maxwell	15	6.25	
6	Langham	30	5.40	
7	Gill	28	6.75	
	D	E	F	G

a) Give the address of any cell that contains currency data.

.... ①

b) What formula would be placed in cell G4 to calculate the gross pay of Raymond?

.... ①

TOTAL 2

23 Describe **two advantages** to a company of using a spreadsheet rather than a calculator to work out how much to pay their staff.

Advantage 1 .... ①

Advantage 2 .... ①

TOTAL 2

24 Explain why automatic data logging is used to record data over **a long period of time**.

....
....
.... ③

TOTAL 3

25 Automatic data logging equipment can be used to create reports in a range of different formats. State **two** types of output suitable for inclusion in a report.

Output 1.. ①

Output 2.. ①

TOTAL 2

26 A large number of companies now issue laptop computers to employees who work from home. State **three** potential problems that could arise from employees taking laptops home.

....

....

....

....

....

.... ⑥

TOTAL 6

27 Office and home environments often have microprocessor-controlled central heating. Briefly describe the **benefits** of microprocessor-controlled central heating.

....

....

....

.... ④

TOTAL 4

28 Bar code systems are a common feature in shops and supermarkets. Each product for sale is given a unique number, e.g. a tin of beans could be labelled YBCD1998.

a) State **two** reasons why bar codes are used.

....

.... ②

b) State the names of **two** data items that are used in bar codes.

Item 1.. ①

Item 2.. ①

c) i) Sometimes the bar code reader fails to read a code correctly. State how the **checkout operator** knows that the bar code has not been read correctly.

....

.... ②

ii) What does a **bar code** contain to help the scanner read it correctly?

....

.... ③

Applications software

iii) What must the checkout operator do if the scanner will not read the bar code?

....

.... ②

TOTAL 11

29 Simple drawing tools are provided with most desktop publishing packages. Six different types of drawing tool are listed below. For each drawing tool, state its use.

a) Pre-set shapes tool

Use .... ①

b) Fill command

Use .... ①

c) Colour palette

Use .... ①

d) Text tool

Use .... ①

e) Freehand drawing tool

Use .... ①

f) Rotation tool

Use .... ①

TOTAL 6

Short-answer questions

1. B   ①
2. B   ①
3. C   ①
4. D   ①
5. B   ①
6. C   ①
7. C   ①
8. A   ①
9. C   ①
10. C   ①
11. A   ①

Long-question answers

1. a) It identifies incorrectly spelt words and suggests alternatives from a list of correctly spelt words. ②

   b) It enables her to place information at the top of the page that she wishes to see at the top of every page. ②

   c) It **automatically** counts the number of words in the document. ①

2. a) Desk-top publishing software ①

   EXAMINER'S TIP

   You would also get a mark here for using a word processor.

   b) Any two from the following list. Can manipulate layout using frames. Can arrange information in columns. Can insert text and images. Can edit text and images. ②

   c) Any three from the following list. Use a scanner to ... Create a bitmap file of the print. Which can be converted into a different format (e.g. GIF, JPEG). Which can be imported into the DTP document. ③

   EXAMINER'S TIP

   Read the question carefully – she is using photographic prints. You will not get marks for using a digital camera as she already has the images. They need to be scanned.

3. Any seven from the following list. Create a template/use a wizard. Use picture frames/text frames. Arrange in columns. Use layout guides/rulers. Create text using a word processor. Create images/logo using a graphics package. Use a scanner to import print pictures. Download digital photographs from a camera. Manipulate pictures using photo-editing software. Import text/graphics/photos into the publishing software. Edit layout by moving/resizing frames. Use Print Preview or WYSIWYG screen to check layout. ⑦

4. A Fully justified; B Justified left; C Centre justified; D Justified right. ④

   EXAMINER'S TIP

   Make sure the examiner knows which term refers to which drawing. If you only know one term it is worth repeating it on all of the drawings as it will be right at least once!

5. Use of letters with mail merge facilities, spelling and grammar checking, greater flexibility in choice of typefaces and layouts used. ③

   EXAMINER'S TIP

   Read the question carefully. It asks for three ways. Do not repeat yourself and remember the context is 'a school office'. Give examples if you can, e.g. mail merge could be used to send individualised standard letters to the parents.

6. Mail merge utilises a file of clients' names and merges these with a standard letter to produce individualised letters automatically. One of the most common uses of mail merge is in the junk mail we receive through our letterboxes. ④

   EXAMINER'S TIP

   There are two parts to this question. Make sure that you answer both.

7. a) She can add the name to the User Dictionary. ①

Applications software

EXAMINER'S TIP

The key word in this question is 'best' friend. If Chloe is writing a large number of letters, she will want to modify the dictionary to avoid the error message. Although 'not using the spell checker' is a viable way of achieving the desired outcome, the examiner will always be looking for an IT solution – after all it is an IT examination!

b) She would ignore the message resulting from a postcode. **1**

c) It would add unnecessary data to the User Dictionary. **2**

EXAMINER'S TIP

The examiner has given you a clue in b) by suggesting it should be a different course of action.

d) Save a document template in which the style, format and type are pre-set, or construct a standard for modification and saving as a new document to suit each particular letter required. **3**

EXAMINER'S TIP

You must mention 'document template' or 'standard letter' to gain marks in this question.

8 a) Change 1: Moving address to the centre of the letter. Feature used: centred text command. **2**
Change 2: Justifying the text so that the left and right borders are parallel. Feature used: Justify text command. **2**
Change 3: Changing the font of the date of the letter. Feature used: format text command. **2**
Change 4: The left margin has been made bigger. Feature used: margin or tab. **2**

EXAMINER'S TIP

Look carefully at the letters to spot the changes before you attempt to answer the question. Sometimes there will be more than one change in a single part of the letter, e.g. the text could be centred and have its font changed, or be made bold.

b) One mark for each correctly underlined section. **4**

16, Springfield Close,
Warrington,
Durham.

19th July 2002

Dear <title> <surname>,

With reference to your recent letter relating to account ,<account>, we regret to inform you that the outstanding balance of <balance> has been refused by your bank.

Please pay the outstanding amount as soon as possible. Any delay will result in additional interest charges.

We look forward to hearing from you soon.

Yours sincerely

Joe Soap, Accounts

EXAMINER'S TIP

Underline all of the sections that appear inside the mail merge markers.

c) The address **1**

9 Advantages: Electronic mail is instant; It can be sent worldwide; It is cheaper than conventional mail as it uses less paper and costs only a local telephone call. Disadvantages: Each recipient needs to have a mail box and a computer system (the computer must be switched on and the user must log on); There is a lack of privacy; You do not have a paper copy to refer to, unless you print it out yourself. **6**

EXAMINER'S TIP

Put your answers in sentences and try to give examples. The question asks for advantages and disadvantages so try to give more than one answer in each case. In this instance the examiner wants three advantages and three disadvantages. It does not say this in the question, but you can tell from the number of marks to be awarded.

10 a) A field is a category of information; a record is a group of related items of information, one for each field. For example, a collection of information about one customer would be a record. **2**

b) She could **search** the database, using criteria TOWN LIKE "Alice Springs". ❷

⑪ a) Bar graph; column graph ❶

b) Any four from the following list. Enter the data onto a spreadsheet. Highlight the data to go into the graph. Select the type of graph. Add axis labels. Add a legend. Format the appearance of the graph. ❹

c) Any four from: Connect to the internet. Open her e-mail software. Insert her friend's e-mail address in the address bar. Attach the file containing the graph to the e-mail. Press send. ❹

⑫ a) Database ❶

b) It could produce a **query** or **search** for all customers whose town on the database is LIKE Halmorden. ❷

c) A **standard letter** is produced using a **word-processor** (do not give named package, e.g. Word). **Field codes** are entered for the parts to be **personalised**. The document is then merged with the **list of names**. The merged documents are then **checked for accuracy** before being **printed**. ❹

⑬ a) C2=B2/40 ❶
b) Replication ❶

c) Using a logic function, accept IF. Using the formula IF(C2>50"Pass","Fail"). ❷

d) Sort the data into order of either mark or percentage. Use the **RANK** function to give each pupil a ranking. ❶

⑭ a) Alphabetically upon surname ❶
b) The final date of birth, for Dates. There are not 31 days in February. ❶

c) Make the field a date field, not an alpha-numeric field. ❶

d) Any reasonable response gains a mark, with one extra mark for the use of the syntax >. E.g. DATE= >01/01/1994 and SEX=M. ❷

e) The field length is the number of characters or numbers that can be typed into the field. ❷

f) A true/false field can hold one or two possible values in numerical or letter form, e.g. Yes or No, 0 or 1. ❷

⑮ a) A distributed database is used on networks of several computers, with each computer sharing part of the data and co-operating in making it available to the user. ❸

b) In a relational database data is stored in a series of tables, each linked to the others by the database management system. This enables the user to view the data in a variety of ways and allows more flexibility in terms of data access and type of query. ❸

Applications software

16) a)

	A	B	C	D
1	Description	Selling price £	Number sold	Sales value
2	ICT textbook	11.75	104	1222.00
3	Food textbook	12.50	94	1175.00
4	Maths textbook	14.00	180	2520.00
5	English textbook	10.75	190	D5 = B5*C5
6	Science textbook	16.50	130	2145.00
7	Total sales		C7 = SUM(C2:C6) or C2+C3+C4+C5+C6	D7 = SUM(D2:D6) or, D2+D3+D4+D5+D6
8				

3

EXAMINER'S TIP

Be careful to give the correct formulae and use abbreviations and functions where they are appropriate. For example, for totals you will get marks for = C2+C3+C4+C5+C6, but you will get an extra mark if you use the function SUM(). The examiner will be looking for your knowledge of functions.

b) The spreadsheet automatically does the calculations for the user, and when the sales totals are changed, the spreadsheet recalculates automatically. It is quick and easy to use and the operator always knows the total sales. **2**

EXAMINER'S TIP

Give a full explanation and remember to use all of the space provided. Try to make your answers specific to the question – the key word in this question is 'formulae'. The examiner is looking for the advantages of building formulae into a spreadsheet.

c) (B5–E5)C5 **1**

EXAMINER'S TIP

The advantage of a spreadsheet is that you do not need to do manual calculations. Examiners will increase the level of difficulty through a question. This section requires a more complex formula than before. Do not simply put in the answer from a manual calculation. The calculation must be automatic when any of the variables are changed.

d) Through the use of Dynamic Data Exchange (DDE) or Object Link Embedding (OLE). **2**

EXAMINER'S TIP

Where you are asked to describe a process towards the end of a question, think of each step you must carry out. Try to explain what type of link you are setting up. Use the correct specialist terms as well as the correct process. Show the examiner what you know, understand and can do.

17) a) Formula: = (B4*C4)+D4+E4 **2**
   b) Method: using the copy command **1**
   c) Formula: = Sum(F4:F8) **2**

EXAMINER'S TIP

Note there is an extra mark in c) for using the function SUM() You would have gained one mark only had you simply answered = F4+F5+F6+F7+F8.

d) A computer model will allow the restaurant to experiment with various options, e.g.:
   - reduced portions to reduce the costs of ingredients
   - larger batch sizes to reduce overheads and thus the cost per unit
   - larger batch sizes to reduce unit costs of ingredients
   - lower pay for the other chef. **4**

EXAMINER'S TIP

A full explanation is required, showing that you understand that a computer model allows you to experiment with various options. Try to make your answers specific to the question – the model allows for a large number of variables. Try to use all of them.

18) A spreadsheet allows you to change one cell and affect the content of a large number of other cells. A spreadsheet can produce diagrams and charts to help you make your

choice. You can use a spreadsheet to ask 'what if' questions and test hypotheses. You can use a spreadsheet for statistical analysis. **⑤**

EXAMINER'S TIP

You will not receive marks for general answers. You must state specifically how the spreadsheet could be used to help model the costs and compare alternatives.

⑲ Analysis of the situation. Design of solutions. Implementation of the system. Training and trials. Evaluation of the system. **⑤**

EXAMINER'S TIP

The stages that you go through in designing and implementing a system are the same whatever the context. Make sure you put the stages in the right order.

⑳ Clip-art is freely available, is copyright free, is easy to access and contains a large amount of pre-drawn material. Its disadvantages are that lots of other people will have used the same images and the Clip-art may not contain the exact picture you want. Drawing your own images means that you have exactly the image you want but you need to be skilled at drawing and it could take a long time. Scanning images has the advantage that you can copy material from any source, so there is a very large amount of resources to draw on. The disadvantages are the cost of the scanner, the size of your computer's memory, and the possibility that you could break the law by using a copyrighted image. **⑦**

EXAMINER'S TIP

The question asks you to compare alternative methods. Therefore you must give at least two methods and, for each, you need to state both the advantages and disadvantages of using that method.

㉑ a) Three records **①**
  b) Six fields **①**
  c) Postcode; phone number; e-mail address; work phone number; date of birth, goods purchased; marital status; religion. **④**

㉒ a) Any F cell from F2 to F7 **①**
  b) Answer: =F4xE4 **①**

㉓ Up to two marks, one for each of the following: fewer staff needed; more accurate; the company gets a printed record; can use the spreadsheet to ask 'what if' questions. **②**

㉔ Give one mark for each valid point up to a maximum of three.
Example answer: You do not need as much human input to collect the results. Electronic data logging is also more accurate and does not rely on people having to remember to take the readings at regular intervals. **③**

EXAMINER'S TIP

Try to mention more than one reason when you are asked this type of question. Often, the mark scheme will allocate marks to the number of points you make. Even though it has four valid points, this answer would only achieve the maximum three marks.

㉕ One mark each for stating any two of the following, or similar: graphs, charts, lists, text. **②**

EXAMINER'S TIP

Do not repeat the same answer, e.g. bar charts and line charts, as you will only gain one mark.

㉖ One mark for stating any of the following, or similar: machines could be lost or stolen; a virus could enter a machine; technical support might be required at home if something went wrong with the machine or software; the company would need to insure the laptops to be taken to employees' homes; the machines might be damaged while in the home; software or data might be damaged if inexperienced users touched the machines; the company would need to introduce strict data security measures as other people would be able to read files. **⑥**

㉗ Marks will be awarded for each of the following points, up to a maximum of four marks. Sensors measure the temperature of rooms exactly. The microprocessor is able to reduce heat if the temperature is too high; increase it if it is too cold. Users can select the times when the system switches on and off. Users can select the temperatures required. **④**

㉘ a) Any two from the following: there is less chance of error; automatic data entry; speed. **②**
  b) Any two from the following: the item code, price, manufacturer, date, country of origin. **②**

EXAMINER'S TIP

The best way to answer this question is to think of what types of output are required to produce an automatic bill and re-order the goods.

c) i)   There is a bleep or flashing light. **2**

   ii)   The bar code is written both ways, so
         that it can be read from either direction,
         and it contains a check digit. **3**

  iii)   Key in the number by hand from the
         number displayed under the bar code. **2**

*This question is based upon a supermarket
checkout. It is not asking for specific computer
knowledge, only general knowledge about the
use of systems.*

29 a)   Use: to draw common shapes accurately,
         e.g. polygons, squares, rectangles and
         circles. **1**

   b)   Use: to fill enclosed shapes with colours,
        tints or shades. **1**

   c)   Use: to select colour, tint or shade for use
        with fill command or other drawing tools. **1**

   d)   Use: to add words and labels. **1**

   e)   Use: to allow you to draw shapes that are
        irregular or not available in the preset
        selection. **1**

   f)   Use: to rotate drawings or text blocks. **1**

*Think about the actions that are described, as
the question might not use the same
commands as the software packages with
which you are familiar. The examiner will select
terms that describe common software features.
You are not expected to be accustomed to
using every available kind of software.*

Networks and communications

To revise this topic more thoroughly, see Chapter 4 in *Letts Revise GCSE Information and Communication Technology Study Guide*.

Try this sample GCSE question and then compare your answer with the Grade C and Grade A model answers on pages 70 and 71.

a Using examples, describe how the use of modern Information and Communication Technology has enabled employees of some companies to work from home.

[8]

b Give a clear description of each of the following network-related terms.

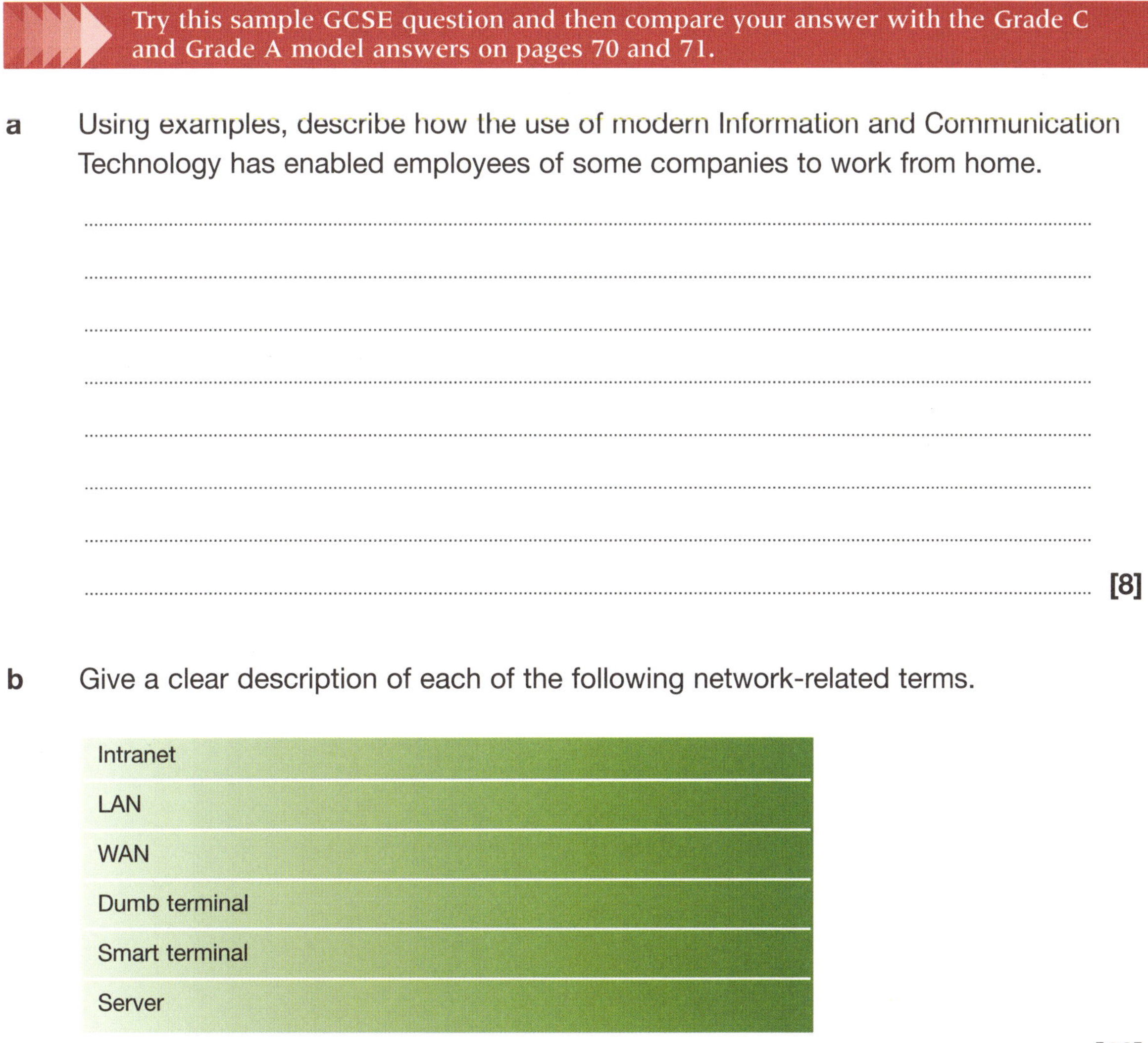

[12]

(Total 20 marks)

GRADE C ANSWER

Ryl has given a very simple example and therefore has not been able to gain higher marks. Three marks awarded.

Ryl has not shown any real knowledge of the information required by this question. The descriptions are weak and simplistic. Ryl is lucky to have been awarded two marks for knowing what LAN and WAN stand for. Four marks awarded.

RYL

a   Typist ✓ The job a typist does can be done on a computer anywhere in the world. ✓ The computer can be linked to the Internet and the typist can type work in and then send it as an e-mail ✓

b

Intranet	A group of computers, as in a school, that can share files ✓
LAN	Local Area Network ✓
WAN	Wide Area Network ✓
Dumb terminal	A computer that cannot talk to others on a network
Smart terminal	A computer that can talk to others on a network
Server	The computer that controls the network ✓

7 marks = Grade C answer

GRADE A ANSWER

Ceri has chosen a relevant occupation and then given at least seven reasons for the role of an accountant to be suitable for home working. She has also mentioned more than just computers and the internet. This broadening of the answer gives the examiner more opportunity to award full marks. Note that the question was about Information Communication Technology, not just computers. Eight marks awarded even though the candidate has made nine points.

CERI

a Accountant. An accountant can do most of his / her work online ✓ on a computer, so he / she does not need to go into an office any more. They can meet their customers at home, or use video conferencing, ✓ they can make phone calls and receive text messages ✓ on their mobile phones, they can use software like spreadsheets ✓ to work out their calculations. This can then be printed and posted, ✓ or e-mailed ✓ to other people and the customers. The Tax Office has a web site that the accountant can access from home and fill in tax returns online. ✓ They can check bank accounts and pay bills over the internet without having to go to the bank. ✓

Ceri has a clear understanding of most of these terms, but has found them difficult to describe. However, the answers are clear enough to allow the examiner to award two marks for each, therefore full marks. Knowledge of the abbreviations has certainly helped. Twelve marks awarded.

b

Term	Description
Intranet	A network of computers that is used in one place like a school where the users can share files but might not have access to the internet. ✓✓
LAN	A network of computers and other equipment like printers that allows users to share information over a short distance, like inside a company or school, usually in the same building. ✓✓
WAN	A network of computers that is spread over greater distances, like all over the world. The internet is a WAN. ✓✓
Dumb terminal	A computer on a network that has no processor of its own so it cannot carry out tasks without using the server. ✓✓
Smart terminal	A computer that has its own processor and memory so that it can work in a network or on its own. ✓✓
Server	The computer that controls the network, holds network software and stores files. ✓✓

20 marks = Grade A answer

Grade booster ⋯⟶ move A to A*

Exam questions are allocated marks according to how many points you are required to make. Try to spend time carefully and ensure you get the key points in the right order, especially when you have to fill in boxes with limited space to write. Try not to cross things out. You may wish to highlight the key points to make it easier for the examiner to see what you want him or her to see.

Short-answer questions

1 A company wishes to connect two site fileservers in different parts of the country using the telephone. They will need a:

A router

B modem

C CD-ROM

D fax machine. ①

2 A Local Area Network (LAN) is a:

A network within a building or site

B network across a city, country or even the world

C network that contains servers across the world

D a network with 2000 or more computers. ①

3 A Wide Area Network (WAN) is a:

A network within a building or site

B network across a city, country or even the world

C network that contains no server

D network with fewer than two computers. ①

4 Networks are useful because:

A no-one can copy your files

B you only need one printer per network

C the computers use less electricity

D each user of the network can access files more easily. ①

5 A peer-to-peer network requires a:

A server

B file server

C workstations

D network interface cards. ①

6 A file server is:

A another name given to a workstation

B a computer that performs a maintenance service for other computers

C a computer that manages and controls the printers on the network

D a computer that stores files that are created by network users. ①

7 A small office has five employees who have a computer each but share two printers. What kind of network would you suggest they install?

A client/server network

B peer-to-peer network

C intranet

D wide area network ①

8 The Protocol used for the internet is:

A INX/UPX

B NetBIOS/NetBEUI

C TCP/IP

D PCI/IP. ①

Long-answer questions

1 In the spaces provided, state what the terms LAN and WAN stand for.

LAN.. ①

WAN... ①

TOTAL 2

2 Name the type of network shown in the illustration.

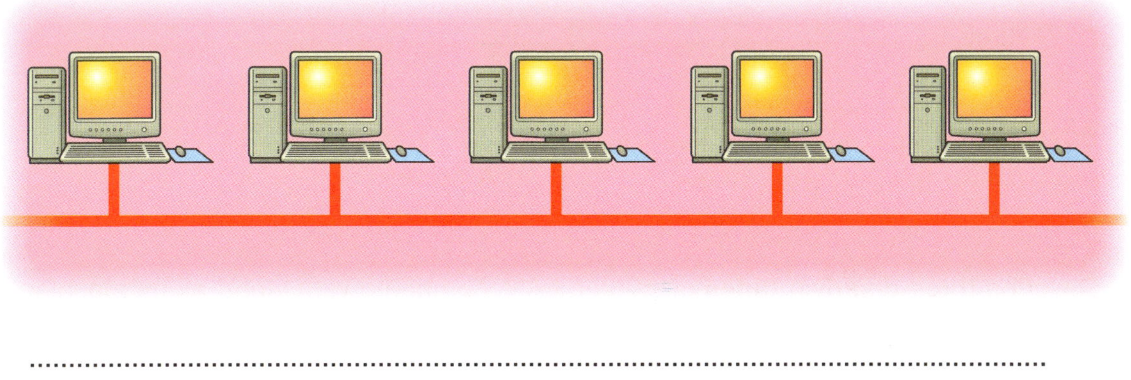

.... ②

TOTAL 2

3 Brights Solicitors has three offices located in different towns. Each branch has a number of computers linked together in a Local Area Network (LAN).

a) What is a LAN?

....

.... ②

b) What is the difference between a LAN and a Wide Area Network?

....

.... ②

c) The LAN is connected together using a line configuration.

Give **one benefit** and **one drawback** of a line configuration.

Benefit ....

.... ②

Drawback..

.... ②

TOTAL 8

4 A large company has a number of offices spread around the country.

a) State whether the offices will be linked together using a LAN (Local Area Network) or WAN (Wide Area Network).

.... ①

b) State one difference between a LAN and a WAN.

....

.... ②

TOTAL 3

5 Describe **three advantages** of using a LAN, compared with stand-alone machines, in a small office environment.

Advantage 1 .... ①

Advantage 2 .... ①

Advantage 3 .... ①

TOTAL 3

6 Describe **three disadvantages** of using a LAN, compared with stand-alone machines, in a small office environment.

Disadvantage 1 .... ①

Disadvantage 2 .... ①

Disadvantage 3 .... ①

TOTAL 3

7 Describe the purpose of a network card.

....

....

....

.... ④

TOTAL 4

8

a) The illustrations below show three different ways a network can be connected. In the spaces provided, name each type of network.

A .... ①

B .... ①

C .... ①

b) Describe the term **hierarchical network**.

....

....

....

.... ④

TOTAL 7

Short-answers questions

1. A
2. A
3. B
4. B
5. D
6. D
7. B
8. C

Long-answer questions

1. LAN = Local Area Network
   WAN = Wide Area Network

EXAMINER'S TIP

Remember you must give exactly the right technical terms to gain marks.

2. Bus network with spurs

EXAMINER'S TIP

It is easy to miss the spurs. Two marks can be awarded in this question and this should give you a clue.

3. a) A group of computers **permanently connected together** usually operated by a **network server**. Each computer can **access** the data stored on the network.

EXAMINER'S TIP

You may wish to highlight the key terms in your answer. This answer is a very good Grade A response using the correct technical language and highlighting the key words.

b) A LAN is a **permanent** network located in the same location (e.g. an office). A WAN is a **temporary** network. LANs are usually connected by **cable**. WANs are usually connected via a **telephone** link.

c) Benefit: line networks are **cheaper** than other networks because **less cable** is needed. Drawback: the system will **slow down** if there are lots of users because all the data flows along the **same cable**.

4. a) A WAN
   b) LAN computers are connected directly by cabling and are normally within the same building; WAN is spread over a wide distance and can use the internet and/or satellite links.

EXAMINER'S TIP

Although this question tells you to state a difference, there are two marks. Try to show that you fully understand the difference and which is which.

5. Costly resources such as printers can be shared. Central backing store can be provided. Software can be shared, making it easier to upgrade. Data can be shared so several people can use the data at the same time. Local e-mail can be sent.

EXAMINER'S TIP

To answer this question, think about the things a small company would want to do, and ways it could save money.

6. Security could be a problem as people can share data. Cabling can be expensive to buy and install. People could waste time sending local e-mails. A virus could easily infect the whole system. People will have to remember passwords and user names.

EXAMINER'S TIP

You can use your answers to the previous question to give you some guidance on how to answer this question.

7. A network card enables a computer to be connected to other computers via cables. It is a small circuit board that can be slotted into connectors on the main circuit board in a computer, called the mother board.

EXAMINER'S TIP

Even if you do not know the answer to this question, the word 'network' should give you a clue to the type of response needed. The number of possible marks will also give you an idea of how much you should write.

8. a) A= ring network; B= Bus network; C= Star network
   b) A hierarchical network has one or more computers that is/are more powerful than the rest. The more powerful computer(s) is called a server. The other computers are called client terminals. The server looks after printing, file management, file maintenance and the peripherals.

EXAMINER'S TIP

You will need to make sure that you use correct technical terms such as server and client.

Networks and communications

To revise this topic more thoroughly, see Chapter 4 in *Letts Revise GCSE Information and Communication Technology Study Guide*.

 Try this sample GCSE question and then compare your answer with the Grade C and Grade A model answers on the pages 78 and 79.

a To connect to the internet, a computer must have access to external communication links. Describe the **advantages** and **disadvantages** of the following which are used to make such links.

Standard 56kbps modem ....

....

....

....

....

.... **[6]**

ISDN 2 ....

....

....

....

....

.... **[6]**

Broadband connection ....

....

....

....

.... **[6]**

b E-mail has become a very popular way of communicating, both in business and private.

State **four advantages** and **four disadvantages** of using e-mail to communicate with a business partner.

Advantages...

....

....

.... **[4]**

Disadvantages ....

....

....

.... **[4]**

c A web site with a universal resource locator, or URL, is viewed on computer using a browser. Access to the internet is provided by an internet service provider, or ISP.

Explain the terms:

Web site..

....

.... **[3]**

Universal resource locator (URL)...

....

.... **[3]**

Browser...

....

.... **[3]**

Internet service provider (ISP). ....

....

.... **[3]**

(Total 38 marks)

GRADE C ANSWER

DARREN

a Standard 56kbps Modem
Advantages: The standard modem is cheap, ✓ easily installed ✓ and connects to a normal telephone line. ✓
Disadvantages: Nobody can use the phone when the computer is online, ✓ connection speed is slower than other methods, ✓ cost of phone call or subscription means it can be expensive to run. ✓

ISDN 2
Advantages: Twice the connection speed of standard modem, ✓ installed like standard modem. ✓
Disadvantages: Costs twice as much to run as a standard modem, nobody can use the phone when the computer is online. ✓

Broadband
Advantages: Very fast connection speed. ✓
Disadvantages: Expensive to run, ✓ not available everywhere. ✓

b Advantages
1. E-mail is fast.
2. E-mail is cheap.
3. You can send pictures with e-mail as an attachment. ✓
Disadvantages
1. You have to be on line to be able to use e-mail.
2. You can receive a lot of junk e-mail or spam. ✓
3. It can take a long time to send a large e-mail.
4. It can take a long time to receive a large e-mail.

c Web site: a web site is a collection of pages that can be seen on computer. The pages are stored on the Internet. ✓ ✓

URL: the address of a web site. ✓

Browser: software used to see a web site.

ISP: company like Virgin that allows you to access the Internet. ✓

18 marks = Grade C answer

Darren obviously has some knowledge of the relative merits of the three systems, but is only able to comment fully upon the modem. The other two systems are not discussed in the same detail, showing a lack of experience with these. However, the answers are well constructed. Breaking the responses down into advantages and disadvantages makes it easier for the examiner to read and award marks. Twelve marks awarded.

Although Darren knows something about e-mail, these answers are not specific enough. They do not reflect an understanding of the question. Terms such as fast and cheap should always be avoided as they are relative, and unless they are qualified with faster than or cheaper than, marks are rarely awarded. Two marks awarded.

Darren has not managed to give enough detail in any of the answers to this question. The response to browser merely repeats the question and therefore gains no marks. Four marks awarded.

Grade booster ---> move a C to a B

Make sure you cover all of the points asked for in the questions. It is easy to miss key marks by getting carried away with your answer while missing other parts of the question which also carry marks.

Try not to repeat the same point over and over again even if you think it matches the next part of the question too. Examiners will only award one mark for each correct point.

The internet and e-mail

GRADE A ANSWER

Steve has a clear understanding of the three terms and is able to write six points about each, therefore being awarded full marks. The style of answer is a little confusing, and the examiner may miss points so the candidate could lose marks because of this. Unlike the Grade C answer, Steve has not tried to describe three advantages and three disadvantages of the systems, but has written at least six points about each, obviously working out that to get 18 marks there must be 18 points shared among three answers. Eighteen marks awarded.

STEVE

a Standard 56kbps Modem

This system uses a device that can be internal, or external to the computer. ✓ It links to the phone line and when a connection is made it dials the internet service provider. ✓ This means that while the computer is online it runs up a phone bill for the time it is using the phone line. ✓ This also means that nobody else can use the phone at the same time. ✓ It is a cheap system to install and most computers are now sold with a modem already fitted. ✓ It is a slow way to connect to the internet ✓ which means some web sites do not run very well.

ISDN 2

ISDN 2 uses digital signals ✓ where a modem has to convert analogue ✓ to digital. This makes ISDN much faster than a modem. ✓ ISDN 2 uses two connections ✓ to speed up transfer even more. It does cost more, however, because you need a special line ✓ and if you use both channels the cost is that of two phone calls ✓ not one. Because ISDN uses the telephone lines it is easy to install but you cannot make a telephone call on the same line when it is connected. ✓

Broadband

Broadband is an always-on connection, which means the computer is permanently connected to the Internet through a special modem or network card. ✓ It does not use the phone line ✓ so you can still make and receive calls when on line. ✓ It is a very fast connection, about 100 times faster than a standard modem. ✓ It is expensive to install ✓ and run because you need special cabling and equipment, ✓ and pay a subscription every month. ✓

This candidate has a clear understanding of the advantages and disadvantages of using e-mail. He has read the question carefully and realised that four advantages and four disadvantages must be mentioned to gain full marks. The answers reflect a good general knowledge of ICT issues. Eight marks awarded.

b Advantages:

It provides a quick way of sending messages all around the world. ✓ People are often happy to send a short e-mail, when they would never send a short letter. ✓ E-mail can be printed out and stored like a normal letter and this can make it easier to record official information. ✓ One e-mail can be sent to hundreds of people at the same time. ✓

Disadvantages:

E-mail can easily be used to send junk mail to thousands of people at the same time. ✓ Viruses can be transmitted by e-mail. ✓ E-mail addresses can be confusing, and you do not always know to whom you send an e-mail or from whom you receive one, because of the address. ✓ E-mail can be read by other people, which causes security problems. ✓

c Website: a collection of web pages, written in a language that can be viewed over the internet. ✓✓

URL: a unique address ✓ where you can find a website by typing in the address. ✓

Browser: a piece of software ✓ in which you can type in a URL or browse the internet. ✓

ISP: providers of internet ✓ and e-mail services. ✓

34 marks = Grade A answer

Grade booster ---> move A to A*

If you intend to use extended writing, plan your answer carefully. You must make enough correct points to gain maximum marks. Always give full explanations, using technical terms and spelling them correctly. Write very clearly and use examples where they will help to illustrate your answers.

QUESTION BANK

Short-answer questions

1 When using a modem, the speed at which you can download files is measured in:

A baud rate or bits per second

B microwaves

C gigabytes

D minutes and seconds. ①

2 The name modem is short for:

A model emulator

B modulator demodulator

C means of downloading electronic mail

D motherboard demodulator. ①

3 The term ISDN refers to:

A integrated system digital network

B integral service digital network

C integrated services digital network

D interconnected supply to digital network. ①

4 The term bandwidth refers to:

A the size of the cable connecting you to the network

B the width of the band holding the cables together

C the resolution of a computer screen

D the transmission capacity of the medium transmitting data across a network. ①

5 You need the following to connect to the internet:

A modem

B CD-ROM

C printer

D mouse. ①

6 FTP stands for:

A file transfer program

B file transmission protocol

C files transferred by post

D file transfer protocol. ①

7 The internet is controlled by:

A the US government

B scientists in Germany

C the UK Government

D no-one. ①

8 IRC stands for:

A Internet Relay Chat

B International Register of Cartoons

C Internet Remote Conversations

D International Real-time Conversations. ①

9 HTML stand for:

A Hyper Textual Mark-up Lingo

B Hyper Text Marking Language

C Hyper Text Mark-up Language

D Home Time Messages Locator. ①

10 You can use communications software to:

A send e-mail over the internet

B multi-task with more than one program open at once

C control a user interface with a mouse

D enter data with a microphone. ①

11 The quickest way to find a known web page is to:

A type in the web page address

B search with a search engine

C leave a message on a web notice board

D search using a directory. ①

12 E-mail allows a user to:

A send messages while off line

B send the same message to a number of people at the same time

C use a mail merge facility

D log on to the internet without a modem. ①

13 If you do not pick up your e-mail for a month:

A it will be deleted automatically

B it will be waiting for you to collect it

C it will be sent back to the sender

D a letter will be sent to you in the post. ①

14 Which of the following is a properly formatted e-mail address?

A STEVE CUSHING @ domain. org. uk

B stevecushing@domain.org.uk

C steve.domain.uk

D Steve_Cushing:domain.org.uk ①

15 E-mail packages usually contain:

A a web browser

B a database package

C an outbox, inbox and address book

D an integrated spreadsheet package. ①

Long-answer questions

1 State **two advantages** of ISDN over a conventional modem and telephone line for accessing the internet.

....

.... ②

TOTAL 2

---

2 A file is taking a long time to download from the internet. Give **three** reasons which might explain this.

Reason 1.. ①

Reason 2.. ①

Reason 3.. ①

TOTAL 3

---

3 The internet is a world-wide network which contains a large amount of data.

a) State **two** ways that the internet could be useful to a book researcher working at home.

Way 1.. ①

Way 2.. ①

b) i) Explain why governments would want to control information on the internet.

....

....

.... ③

ii) Explain why people are **opposed** to this type of control.

....

....

.... ③

TOTAL 8

4 Rogers Electrical have decided to advertise on the internet.

a) State **three benefits** to a company like Rogers of advertising on the internet.

Benefit 1 .... ①

Benefit 2 .... ①

Benefit 3 .... ①

b) Name **one** piece of software that the company will need to sell its goods over the internet.

.... ①

c) The company finds that some customers do not like to use their credit cards to pay for goods on the internet.

Give **one** reason why.

....

.... ②

d) State **two** reasons why the company's customers might prefer to use e-mail as opposed to telephoning or writing to the company.

Reason 1.. ①

Reason 2.. ①

e) In order to make use of a web site and e-mail facility, all customers will need a particular piece of hardware connected to their computer. Name the hardware.

.... ①

TOTAL 9

5 Newspaper editors gather articles from reporters working across the world. Most articles are written using a word processor. Once written, the articles are transferred electronically.

a) Describe the steps needed to transfer an article electronically.

....

....

.... ③

b) Describe how a desktop publishing package can be used to convert the articles into a newspaper incorporating pictures as well as text.

....

....

....

....

....

.... ⑥

TOTAL 9

Short-answer questions

1	A	**2**	B
3	C	**4**	D
5	A	**6**	D
7	D	**8**	A
9	C	**10**	A
11	A	**12**	B
13	B	**14**	B
15	C		

Long-answer questions

1 It is faster; data can be compressed; access is faster. **2**

2 Slow modem. Large file. Heavy traffic on the internet. Slow server used to store the file on the internet. **3**

3 a) Any sensible reasons would be allowed – one mark for brief responses and two marks for expanded points. Way 1: Access to other people's research papers. Way 2: Can use the web to send out questions and make contact with experts. **2**

EXAMINER'S TIP

Think about the internet and its use as a communications system. A researcher needs access to information.

  b) i) To prevent illegal material being available. To control pornographic and other unsuitable material. To avoid the illegal transfer of copyright material. To stop libel. To control terrorists. **3**

    ii) The internet provides a freely available source of information. Private mail should not be censored. Censorship could be on political grounds. It is difficult to enforce and costly to incorporate. **3**

EXAMINER'S TIP

When questions are given this many marks the examiner usually wants more than one reason, even when this is not stated in the question.

4 a) One mark for each of the following, or similar: wider audience is reached; low cost compared with other advertising methods; easy way of obtaining market research; bigger turnover; easy to update your advertisement; advertising can be interactive. **3**

b) Either communications software or browser software. **1**

EXAMINER'S TIP

Do not mention actual software by brand name. You will not get marks for saying Internet Explorer or Netscape as these are brands not generic terms. Watch out for this in all of the software answers you give.

c) Any one of the following: they could be afraid that criminals will get their credit card number; they could fear that they could pay and the company will not deliver the goods; they could be afraid that criminals could hack into their personal details. **2**

d) Any two of the following: e-mail is faster; cheaper; can be used 24 hours per day; phone might be engaged; e-mail provides a written record. **2**

e) Either modem or ISDN link. **1**

5 a) Any three of the following: modem link to telephone line; load software; dial up number; type access code; type password; load text file and transmit. **3**

EXAMINER'S TIP

In this type of question you must show your knowledge by stating the equipment requirements, e.g. telephone and modem.

b) For example, you could import the text from the article and import scanned or photographed TIF images into the text, change the font, layout, colour and create frames. **6**

EXAMINER'S TIP

This type of question requires short sentences that clearly show how to change basic text into a newspaper article. You must read the question clearly and state how you could add pictures as well as the text. Try to be concise in your answer and add technical terms where appropriate.

Data, accuracy and security

To revise this topic more thoroughly, see Chapters 3, 6 and 7 in *Letts Revise GCSE Information and Communication Technology Study Guide*.

 Try this sample GCSE question and then compare your answer with the Grade C and Grade A model answers on pages 87–89.

Rogers Electrical Company uses a database to record the details of all its mail order customers.

a The database below is an address book file used by Rogers Electrical.

ID	Surname	First name	Dear	Address	Postcode
001	Jones	Brian	Brian	5 Field Crescent	SY14BA
002	Brown	Joanna	Jo	7 Field Close	BB55YX
003	Patel	Sanjay	Sanj	14 Bristol Drive	CD24YV
004	Williams	Stuart	Stew	7 Northfield	WA45RT
005	Cooper	Mary	Mary	42 Bishops Lane	SD78TG
006	Makefast	Robert	Bob	271 Hillview	SW45RD

(i) How many records are shown on the database?

.... [1]

(ii) For each record, how many fields are shown?

.... [1]

(iii) State the name of a field that contains numeric data.

.... [1]

(iv) Give the name of a field that uses alphanumeric data.

.... [1]

(v) The reference column is used as a key field. State the purpose of a key field.

.... **[1]**

(vi) The postcode entries are typed using an input mask. State **two advantages** and **two disadvantages** of using an input mask.

....

....

....

.... **[4]**

b Explain why security is important to Rogers Electrical Company's information system and its users.

....

....

....

....

....

....

....

.... **[8]**

c Explain how the following methods could help a user to maintain the security of computer files:

- encryption
- firewalls
- passwords.

Encryption...

....

.... **[3]**

Firewalls...

....

.... **[3]**

Passwords...

....

.... **[3]**

d Explain why it is important for Rogers Electrical to validate data entries.

....

....

....

.... **[4]**

e Describe what effect the Data Protection Act 1998 has had on the misuse of electronic data.

....

....

....

....

....

.... **[6]**

(Total 36 marks)

GRADE C ANSWER

Zara has shown a basic knowledge of database work, but as the question gets slightly more difficult, the candidate finds it more difficult to supply a suitable answer. Four marks awarded.

Zara has managed to achieve only three of the marks available for this question. The answers do not reflect a real knowledge of the subject and could be given by anybody with a general knowledge of computing. Zara also strays into why the health service would need security when the question is about a company called Rogers Electrical.

Zara has some understanding of the meanings of the words but does not really know what the three methods do or how they do it. Five marks awarded.

Zara is able to give only one reason in answer to this question, with one appropriate example. Two marks awarded.

Zara has shown some understanding of the DPA, but has only been able to give one example to support her answer. The examiner has therefore only been able to award one of the potential six marks. More detailed knowledge is needed to achieve the higher marks.

ZARA

a   (i)   6 ✔
     (ii)   6 ✔
     (iii)   ID ✔
     (iv)   Postcode ✔
     (v)   To keep the data in order.
     (vi)   So that you can type in only the postcode.

b   It is important to keep files and information secure, because some of the data might be personal or private. ✔ For example, when you buy something on the Internet, you hand over your credit card details. If the web site is not secure, with a padlock in the bottom corner, it means someone else can read your details and may be able to use your card illegally. ✔ Medical records are also stored on computers. These must be kept safe as they often contain personal information. ✔

c   Encrypting a file means jumbling it up so that other people cannot read it unless they know how to decrypt it. ✔✔
A firewall is a piece of software that stops viruses getting onto a computer. ✔✔
A password is a code that a user types in to protect files. ✔

d   It is important to type data in correctly so that information that is stored is correct. ✔ For example, if a medical record were incorrectly entered, the wrong operation could be carried out. ✔

e   The Data Protection Act has meant that it is illegal to hold data about somebody without them knowing about it. ✔ People can take companies to court if the company has stored data without telling the person.

15 marks = Grade C answer

Grade booster ····▶ move a C to a B

Questions often use abbreviations. In your revision you must make sure that you learn not only what the letters of the abbreviations stand for but what the device or definition means. For example, the term URL stands for universal resource locator. However, this actually means an address of a site on the internet. Question papers often follow in this way, where an answer to the first section of a question is used in the second part of the question. You can tell that the two parts of the question relate to each other by the numbering of the questions. Exam boards will use Roman numerals (i, ii, iii, iv) to show the two sections are tightly related, and lower case letters (a, b, c, d) to show that two sections are linked.

Azhim has a clear understanding of the use of databases. Where one mark is awarded for a correct answer he has written the minimum required. Where more marks are awarded, sentences have been used to convey a clear understanding. Nine marks awarded.

Azhim has thought about the answer and has broken it down into different sections: hardware and software. The structure has helped to achieve full marks as it has organised the answer. It is also much easier for the examiner to read. Eight marks awarded.

Azhim has a clear understanding of the three terms and is able to state at least three points about each. The candidate is obviously aware of the security process and how it is used in an information system. Nine marks awarded.

AZHIM

a   (i)   6 ✓

     (ii)   6 ✓

     (iii)   ID ✓

     (iv)   Postcode ✓

     (v)   This gives an order to the data, so that when it is searched or ranked it can easily be re-sorted into its original order. ✓

     (vi)   Advantages: The person entering the data must type in two letters followed by two numbers followed by two letters. ✓ The text entered will always appear as capitals. ✓ Disadvantages: If the postcode of the address does not match the input mask it cannot be entered. ✓ It does not check that what is typed in is a postcode. ✓

b   Security is an important aspect to be considered with any information system. The hardware: Computer equipment is expensive, so it must be kept securely; rooms and equipment must be locked up when not in use. ✓✓ Passwords and logins are often used to stop unauthorised use of equipment, and this helps to avoid hazards like viruses and other damage. ✓✓ The software: Files must be protected with passwords, as they are often personal and contain data that you wouldn't want someone else to read. ✓✓ E-mail and other methods of transporting information over the internet must be carried out through secure connections as this avoids hackers getting hold of your e-mail or credit card number and using it illegally. ✓✓

c   Encryption: data is translated into a secret code. The only way of reading a secret code is if you have a key. The key must be changed regularly so that anyone trying to hack in and read the data will be unable to do so. ✓✓✓ A firewall is a piece of software that is used in a network to protect it from unauthorised access. All information passing from one machine to another goes through the firewall, where it is checked for viruses or other things that breach the security. ✓✓✓

A password is a code of letters and numbers that should be kept secret. It should be changed regularly. It is usually used to stop unauthorised access to certain files. Access to the files cannot be gained without the correct password. ✓✓✓

Azhim has given four clear reasons to support the answer, including knowledge of the Data Protection Act. The examiner is therefore able to award full marks. Four marks awarded.

d   Data must be entered accurately. To ensure this, computers can have automatic validation checks. ✓ If data is incorrectly entered, all sorts of problems can occur. For example, if a postcode is wrong, anything to be sent by post might go to the wrong address. ✓ If credit card details are not correct, the wrong person may be charged for goods that someone has bought.
The Data Protection Act also means that all data stored about a person must be accurate, ✓ so incorrect data can be illegal. ✓

Azhim has obviously revised and prepared well for the examination. The answer shows an understanding of the DPA and how the misuse of data is controlled by it. He has been awarded full marks because he has at least six clear points. He could have achieved similar marks with fewer points by giving examples of how the point affects the misuse of data. Six marks awarded.

e   The Data Protection Act came into force to protect the individual from the misuse of data, ✓ this means that any data recorded about an individual must adhere to certain rules: the data must be processed fairly, ✓ must be for lawful purposes, ✓ must be accurate, ✓ must be destroyed after use, ✓ must be secure. ✓

36 marks = Grade A answer

Grade booster ····⟩ move A to A*

It is important to read the questions carefully and try to put one point in your answer for each mark that can be awarded. If the question asks for a stated answer it usually requires one word or a very short sentence. If it asks for a description, the examiner will expect to see longer sentences or a short paragraph. An explanation may involve sketching, as well as text, and therefore the answer tends to be a little longer.

QUESTION BANK

Short-answer questions

1 Key field is a:

  A term used to describe a field that is unique

  B text only field

  C number only field

  D key place name. ①

2 A field holds:

  A just one piece of data

  B a number of records

  C a hyperlink

  D RAM (random access memory). ①

3 The term ASCII refers to:

  A numeric data

  B a formatting code

  C a picture

  D a text character code. ①

Long-answer questions

1 Describe **three** important considerations when designing a unique code.

  Consideration 1 .... ①

  Consideration 2 .... ①

  Consideration 3 .... ①

TOTAL 3

2 Barry Blank wishes to set up a database to store details of his large DVD collection.

  a) Identify four categories of information on which Barry will wish to obtain information.

  Category 1 .... ①

  Category 2 .... ①

  Category 3 .... ①

  Category 4 .... ①

  b) For each type of information give a suitable field name and a data type.

Category	Field Name	Data Type

  ⑥

  c) Explain **one** method of validating entries in **one** of the fields you have identified.

  ....

  .... ②

TOTAL 12

3 The school office administrator is setting up a database. The table below shows the nature of the data they wish to enter into the database. For each data item, state the field type they would use.

Field name	Length	Field type
Date	8	
First name	12	
Family name	12	
Boy/girl	1	
Date of birth	2	
Address	18	

⑥

TOTAL 6

4 The owner of a shop selling security systems uses a database for stock control. Part of the database is shown below:

Reference	Description	Stock	Minimum level	Order quantity	Replace	Supplier reference
001	Key blank	11	10	20	n	K003
002	Lock	10	15	20	y	K003
003	Bell	15	10	30	n	B004
004	Horn	12	10	10	n	B004
005	Light	8	12	50	y	B004
006	Bell push	15	20	50	y	K003

a) What is a primary key field in a database?

.... ①

b) Identify the primary key field in the database shown.

.... ①

c) Give the reference of the stock items that need to be re-ordered.

.... ①

d) State whether the items that need to be re-ordered are all from the same supplier.

.... ①

e) The database shown uses the following query language: field, comparison, value / field. The search description = horn would find the item reference 004.

i) Write down the query that would find all items supplied by Supplier B004.

.... ①

ii) Using logical operators to combine simple queries, write down the query that will show all of the items that need to be re-ordered as their stock levels are too low.

....

.... ②

TOTAL 7

5 A school library uses a database to record book loans. Part of the database is shown below.

Reference	Book	Out	On loan to	Author
001	A Dog So Small	Y	103	Phillipa Pearce
002	The Sword in the Stone	Y	63	T.H. White
003	Dragon Slayer	N		Rosemary Sutcliffe
004	Alice in Wonderland	N		Lewis Carroll
005	The Tale of Squirrel Nutkin	N		Beatrix Potter
006	Burglar Bill	N		Allan Ahlberg

a) Name the unique field in the database.

.... ①

b) Name the type of field that the **Out** field is in the database and state why it is this type of field.

....

.... ②

c) Describe the steps that the school librarian must take to keep the database accurate and up to date.

....

....

....

....

.... ⑤

d) The school librarian uses the database to send out automatic reminders when books are late. What field, that is not shown, must the database contain to enable her to do this?

.... ①

e) Describe **one advantage** and **one disadvantage** of using a computer-based system as opposed to a manual card system in the library.

Advantage..

....

.... ③

Disadvantage..

....

.... ③

TOTAL 15

6 a) Briefly describe the term **computer virus**.

....

....

.... ③

b) Write down two methods you could use to stop your machine being affected by computer
viruses.

....

....

.... ③

TOTAL 6

7 Network managers usually restrict the use of floppy disks. This helps to prevent the system
from getting infected by a virus.

a) What is a computer virus?

....

.... ②

b) State **two** precautions that a network manager could take to prevent a virus entering the
system.

Precaution 1 .... ①

Precaution 2 .... ①

Your school will have a way of dealing with this problem. Simply state what this is.

TOTAL 4

8 Fletcher-Boycott Financial Services stores confidential information about its customers on
its computer system. The company wishes to prevent unauthorised staff from gaining
access to the data.
Describe how the business could achieve this.

....

....

.... ③

TOTAL 3

9 Describe ways in which computers can be misused, leading to legal and moral problems.

....

....

....

....

....

....

....

.... ⑧

TOTAL 8

10 George McTavish works for a private detective agency. On Monday morning he opens the office to discover that his computer has been left switched on. George suspects that someone has been using his computer over the weekend.

a) Why might George be worried about this?

....

....

.... ③

b) Identify **two** things that George could do to protect the files on his computer.

Protection 1 .... ①

Protection 2 .... ①

TOTAL 5

11 Samantha is married with three children. She works as a secretary in a local company. She owns her own house. She has a mortgage of £40000. She enjoys reading and is a member of a mail-order book club. She shops at the local supermarket and usually pays for her shopping with a credit card.

a) Use the information about Samantha to list **four** facts about her that could be stored in a computer database.

Fact 1.. ①

Fact 2.. ①

Fact 3.. ①

Fact 4.. ①

b) Explain the **difference** between information and data.

....

.... ②

TOTAL 6

12 Orinoco.com sells books on the internet. Customers order books by entering data onto an on-line form. Customers can pay for the books using their credit cards.

a) Apart from credit card details, list **four** items of data that the forms might ask the customer to give.

Item 1.. ①

Item 2.. ①

Item 3.. ①

Item 4.. ①

b) Which method of validation will be used to ensure that a valid credit card number has been entered?

.... ①

c) Explain how this method works.

....

.... ②

d) Some fields on the form have to be completed by the customer.

Name the type of validation that will be used to make sure that information has been entered.

.... ①

e) Give **one** drawback of using data validation.

.... ①

f) The customer might be asked to enter some information twice. Explain why.

....

.... ②

TOTAL 11

13 A bank stores a large amount of information on computer files. Discuss the possible consequences for a customer of inaccurate data being held on the bank's computer files.

....

....

....

.... ④

TOTAL 4

14 Whenever the customer joins a reward scheme and gives their name and address to a shop assistant, the information will be held on a computer database. The Data Protection Act protects the customer from misuse of this data.

a) Give **three** rules relating to customer information which the shop must obey.

Rule 1.. ①

Rule 2.. ①

Rule 3.. ①

b) Give **three** examples of data that do not need to be registered under the Data Protection Act.

Example 1... ①

Example 2... ①

Example 3... ①

TOTAL 6

15 A doctor's surgery uses a computerised system. The surgery's database contains personal information of a confidential nature.

a) Name **three** items of personal data, other than name and address, that the surgery might hold about its patients.

Item 1.. ①

Item 2.. ①

Item 3.. ①

b) How could the surgery protect and secure the data?

....

.... ②

c) Would the surgery need to register under the Data Protection Act?

.... ①

TOTAL 6

16 A new company, Alpha, gains data by carrying out a street survey. It constructs a database containing names, addresses, family details, socio-economic groupings and buying habits.

It registers the information in accordance with the Data Protection Act.

a) Is the company acting in accordance with the law?

.... ①

b) A telesales company offers to purchase the data from Alpha. Under what circumstances would it be legal for Alpha to sell them the data?

....

.... ②

TOTAL 3

ANSWERS ON PAGE 99 ANSWERS ON PAGE 99 ANSWERS ON PAGE 99 ANSWERS ON PAGE 99

Short-answer questions

1. A

2. A

3. D

Long-answer questions

1. The code must be easy to use, or operators will not be able to remember it. Codes should always be the same length. This enables validation checks to take place. Codes should not be too short, especially where security is an issue. **(3)**

> **EXAMINER'S TIP**
>
> *Questions on entering data are often hidden within other general questions on database or spreadsheet software.*

2. a) Any four from: name of film; director; year released; length; style/genre; certificate; rating (e.g. marks out of ten). **(4)**

   b) One mark for each appropriate answer e.g.
   Name: text
   Director: text
   Year: date or number
   Length: number (integer)
   Style: text
   Certificate: text (or alphanumeric)
   Rating: text or number **(6)**

   c) Two marks for a validation formula. One mark for a general description.
   e.g. Year>1900, e.g. Certificate LIKE "PG" OR "U" OR "18" **(2)**

3.

Field Name	Length	Field Type
Date	8	Date
First Name	12	Alphanumeric
Surname	12	Alphanumeric
Boy-Girl	1	True/false
Age	2	Numeric
Address	18	Alphanumeric

(6)

> **EXAMINER'S TIP**
>
> *You must use the correct terminology for the software you use and do not simply state alphanumeric in all of the fields.*

4. a) It is a field which uniquely identifies a record. **(1)**

   b) The key field is Reference. **(1)**

> **EXAMINER'S TIP**
>
> *Even if you used this information in the previous section, e.g. 'A field which uniquely identifies a record. For example, in this database it is the Reference field', give the answer again. Do not expect the Examiner to notice that you have answered the question correctly in the wrong place.*

   c) 002, 005 and 006 **(1)**

> **EXAMINER'S TIP**
>
> *You must list all of the references here to get one mark.*

   d) No **(1)**

> **EXAMINER'S TIP**
>
> *This type of question is set to see if you understand the structure of a database and can read information from one. Remember to use the exact field names shown in the sample database and give the correct numbers. Failure to do so can cost marks.*

   e) i) Supplier Reference, B004. **(1)**

   ii) Stock < Min Level AND Replace = Y
   One mark for each component:
   Stock, < Min level, AND, Replace = Y **(2)**

> **EXAMINER'S TIP**
>
> *Where large numbers of marks have been allocated for this type of question, the marks have been split up so that each piece of the search formula has been given a mark. Make sure you read the question carefully and state the exact formula using the full names of the field.*

5. a) Reference **(1)**

   b) True/false field. The library must have a unique number for each book and it can only be in or out. **(2)**

   c) Delete books that are old, destroyed, stolen or lost. Carry out a regular stock check. Make sure every book that leaves the library is entered into the database to prevent theft. Check that all the books taken are entered correctly. **(5)**

d) Date ❶
e) One of the following in each case. Advantages for the librarian: speed of booking out/in; automatic records; ease of use. Disadvantages for the school: Cost of equipment; cost of training; need for staff training; need to add bar codes to books. ❻

❻ a) A computer virus is a program that can corrupt other applications software and computer operating systems. It is usually transferred from one computer to another by disk or e-mail. ❸
b) One mark for stating any of the following, or similar: use virus checking software; do not log on to the network, do not load data from unreliable floppy disks; do not let anyone else use your computer. ❸

❼ a) A virus is a piece of software that corrupts other software and is transmitted from one computer to another. ❷

b) Any two from the following; do not let anyone use disks; scan the disks first using a dedicated antivirus machine; use antivirus software or a virus scanner. ❷

❽ Three from the following list; protect files using usernames and passwords. Restrict user access to the files by setting different access rights; keep the files on a separate network and restrict physical access, e.g. by locking doors; keep the files separate by using firewalls. ❸

❾ Marks will be awarded, by awarding one mark for any of the following points made in the answer:
illegal downloading of software; illegal use of personal data; fraud; illegal use of pornographic images; spreading viruses; hacking into other people's computers; selling personal information; illegally accessing personal data. ❽

❿ a) Any three from the following: someone might have **viewed** his files; someone might have **copied** his files; someone might have **deleted** or altered some files; someone might have planted a **virus** on the computer. ❸
b) Any two from the following; install a username and password; install anti-virus software; make files read-only; keep back-up copies of important files. ❷

⓫ a) Owner; £40 000 mortgage; credit card; reads books. ❹

b) Data has no context. Information is data in a context. ❷

⓬ a) Name, address, books to be ordered, e-mail address. ❹

b) Check digit ❶

c) The final digit of the number is calculated using a **formula** based on all the previous digits. If this digit is the **same** as the digit entered by the customer then the number is valid. **❷**

d) Presence check **❶**

e) It only makes sure that the data is sensible, not that it is accurate. **❶**

f) So that the computer can **verify** that the information has been entered correctly. So that the computer can **compare the two entries** to see if they are the same. **❷**

❸ Statements could be delivered to the wrong address; money could be credited to the wrong account. You could be told you were overdrawn when you weren't. People could draw your money out by mistake or intent. **❹**

❹ a) Any three from the following: the data must be obtained lawfully and fairly; it must be kept secure; it should be destroyed when no longer required; it must not be excessive; you must be allowed to see any data kept about you, on request; the shop must register and use the data only for registered purposes. **❸**

b) Any three from the following: data stored for wage purposes; data where the individual cannot be identified; data held for personal purposes; data about members of private clubs where all members have agreed to store the data. **❸**

❺ a) Any three of the following: age; allergies; weight; details of immunisation; details of past illnesses; addictions; contraceptives used. **❸**

b) By having passwords or encryption, and keeping computer files secure, e.g. locking the room the computer is in, barring the windows and installing an alarm system. **❷**

c) Yes **❶**

❻ a) Yes **❶**

b) It would be legal for Alpha to sell the data provided that the company had registered under the Act the fact that it intended to sell the data. **❷**

CHAPTER 8

Designing systems

To revise this topic more thoroughly, see Chapter 5 in *Letts Revise GCSE Information and Communication Technology Study Guide*.

 Try this sample GCSE question and then compare your answers with the Grade C and Grade A model answers on the next page.

The manager of a library wishes to design a new security system for administering stock. The existing system must first be analysed and evaluated.

Describe the steps that should be taken in analysing a system.

....

....

....

....

....

.... [6]

(Total 6 marks)

GRADE C ANSWER

Emma has not been able to show much knowledge through this answer. It is very simplistic and does not cover the three points well. Three marks awarded.

> EMMA
>
> The manager should carry out a survey to find out what each person does already. ✔ The manager should draw up a list of all stages of the problem. ✔ He/she should work out the cost of each stage. ✔

3 marks = grade C answer

Grade booster ⋯⟩ move a C to a B

Questions about designing systems will often ask a candidate to list or describe a number of items from a section of the design process. It is therefore important that you clearly understand what is required at each stage of designing a system. All examination boards have a similar definition of the design process:

- analysis of the problem
- design of a solution to the problem
- implementation of the solution, and testing
- evaluation of the process and the solution.

Within each of the stages there are a number of activities that must be carried out. Most of the answers will be of a general nature as this process can be applied to any information systems problem.

GRADE A ANSWER

Chris has obviously revised this area well. She has been able to write a clear explanation of how to analyse a system in general. At least six points have been covered and therefore full marks are awarded.

> CHRIS
>
> The manager should carry out research on the current system, ✔ and work out what information the new system needs. ✔ The manager should then analyse what computer processing will be required ✔ and other constraints of the system, including costs. ✔ The next stage is to break the system into steps ✔ and produce a block diagram or system flow chart, ✔ listing what methods of data capture, hardware and software are already being used. ✔ They should also carry out a survey of people's opinions, and what they think the new system should do.

6 marks = Grade A answer

Grade booster ⋯⟩ move A to A*

To gain A* marks you will need to relate your answer to specific examples. Always try to illustrate your answers and remember to relate the examples specifically to the question. In system design questions you can always compare a manual and computer-based system to make a point.

Short-answer questions

1 Name the main steps involved in developing an information system.

A specification, design, and testing

B programming, design, and testing

C analysis, system design, implementation and testing

D design, programming, test, implement ①

2 What areas need to be considered in the design process?

A only hardware and software

B inputs, outputs, file design, hardware, and software

C maintenance, reliability, and upgradeability

D only user documentation ①

3 What is parallel running?

A the new system is introduced alongside the existing system

B the new system is introduced and users start operating it

C users continue operating the old system

D the new system is left on for a long time ①

4 User guides are used:

A for technical support

B to enable any printer to be connected to the network

C to explain how to run the system, enter data, save, print, etc.

D to explain how to build the computer ①

Long-answer questions

1 Explain in detail how a computer-aided learning system could help a child learn simple arithmetic.

....

....

....

....

....

....

....

.... ⑧

TOTAL 8

2 An electricity company processes all customer bills once a month. Customers whose name begins with A are processed on the first day of the month. Customers whose name begins with B on the second, and so on.

a) What is the name for this type of processing?

.... ①

b) The electricity company stores customer records in a database using a sequential access system. Explain what is meant by sequential access.

....

....

.... ③

TOTAL 4

3 What does this symbol mean when used on a system flow diagram?

.... ①

TOTAL 1

4 Harris Bakeries wishes to update its computer system. It employs a systems analyst to manage the introduction of the new system.

a) Give **one** reason why the computer system may require updating.

.... ①

b) The analyst decides to identify the problems with the existing system.

Give **two** methods that the analyst could use to obtain this information.

Method 1 .... ①

Method 2 .... ①

c) The analyst decides to test the new system using **invalid data**.

What is invalid data?

.... ①

d) The analyst produces a **user's guide** for the new system.

Give **two** pieces of information that should be included in the user's guide.

....

.... ②

e) The analyst decides to introduce the new system in one go, but for a period of three weeks the old system will be kept running as well.

i) Give the name of this type of system installation.

.... ①

ii) Give **one benefit** and **one drawback** of this type of installation.

Benefit .... ①

Drawback.. ①

TOTAL 9

5 State the **seven** main stages of a system's life cycle.

Stage 1 .... ①

Stage 2 .... ①

Stage 3 .... ①

Stage 4 .... ①

Stage 5 .... ①

Stage 6 .... ①

Stage 7 .... ①

TOTAL 7

6 Describe **three** tests that a spreadsheet system could be subjected to during the implementation process.

Test 1 ....

.... ②

Test 2 ....

.... ②

Test 3 ....

.... ②

TOTAL 6

7 All systems need to be maintained. Maintenance is often classified under the following headings:

- corrective maintenance
- adaptive maintenance
- perfective maintenance.

Briefly describe each type of maintenance.

Corrective maintenance...

.... ②

Adaptive maintenance...

.... ②

Perfective maintenance...

.... ②

TOTAL 6

8 Describe the **advantages** and **disadvantages** of shopping electronically.

....

....

....

....

....

....

....

.... ⑧

TOTAL 8

9 The police use a computer database to help them identify criminals and prevent future crime.

a) Name **two** ways in which the police might use computer-stored data to prevent crime.

Way 1.. ①

Way 2.. ①

b) Name **two** ways in which the police might use computer-stored data to solve crimes.

Way 1.. ①

Way 2.. ①

TOTAL 4

QUESTION BANK ANSWERS

Short-answer questions

1. D

2. B

3. A

4. C

Long-answer questions

1. The software puts questions up on the screen. The child keys in an answer. If the answer is correct, the system congratulates the child, often with a smiling face, or some other graphic that encourages the child. Depending on how many answers the child gets right, the program progresses to more difficult sums. If the child gets the answer wrong, the system sets easier sums. **8**

2. a) Batch processing **1**
   b) Sequential access data is where the records are stored one after the other, e.g. on a magnetic tape, where the records are in some logical order. **3**

3. Manual input **1**

4. a) One from: insufficient memory to store all the data; too slow (processor speed); programs are out of date; no longer do what the bakery wants them to do. **1**
   b) Any two from: interview users; observe users; monitor the performance of the system (e.g. speed of processing instructions); study documents such as error reports. **2**
   c) Data that the analyst knows the system should reject. **1**
   d) Any two from: installation information; how to use the software; tutorials; how to solve simple problems. **2**
   e) i) Parallel implementation/installation. **1**
      ii) Benefits: new system can be tested quickly; problems with the new system will not affect the running of the business. Drawbacks: all tasks need to be done twice; creates more work for the bakery staff. **2**

5. Analysis, design, testing, implementation, documentation, evaluation, maintenance. **7**

6. Data with errors could be entered to see if the system picks up the errors during validation; a large amount of data could be entered to see if the system copes with the volume; extreme data could be entered to try out the range checks; different calculations could be performed over and over again to check consistency of results. **6**

7. Corrective maintenance is used to correct or fix errors that show up once the system is in use. Adaptive maintenance is used to make changes to the system where, in use, the requirements have changed. Perfective maintenance is used to make the system better than it was in the first place. **6**

8. Advantages: you do not have to go out; you can compare prices easily; you can shop at any time of day or night; you do not have to carry the shopping; prices are often lower. Disadvantages: no human contact; you could experience security problems when paying; you cannot look at and touch the goods before buying them; you have to have the technology to be able to shop electronically; not all types of goods are available electronically. **8**

9. a) Way 1: Monitoring known criminals. **1**
      Way 2: Patrolling 'black spots' (areas where there is a lot of crime). **1**
   b) Way 1: Matching fingerprint samples. **1**
      Way 2: DNA profiles and information on suspects' past movements. **1**

To revise this topic more thoroughly, see Chapter 8 in *Letts Revise GCSE Information and Communication Technology Study Guide*.

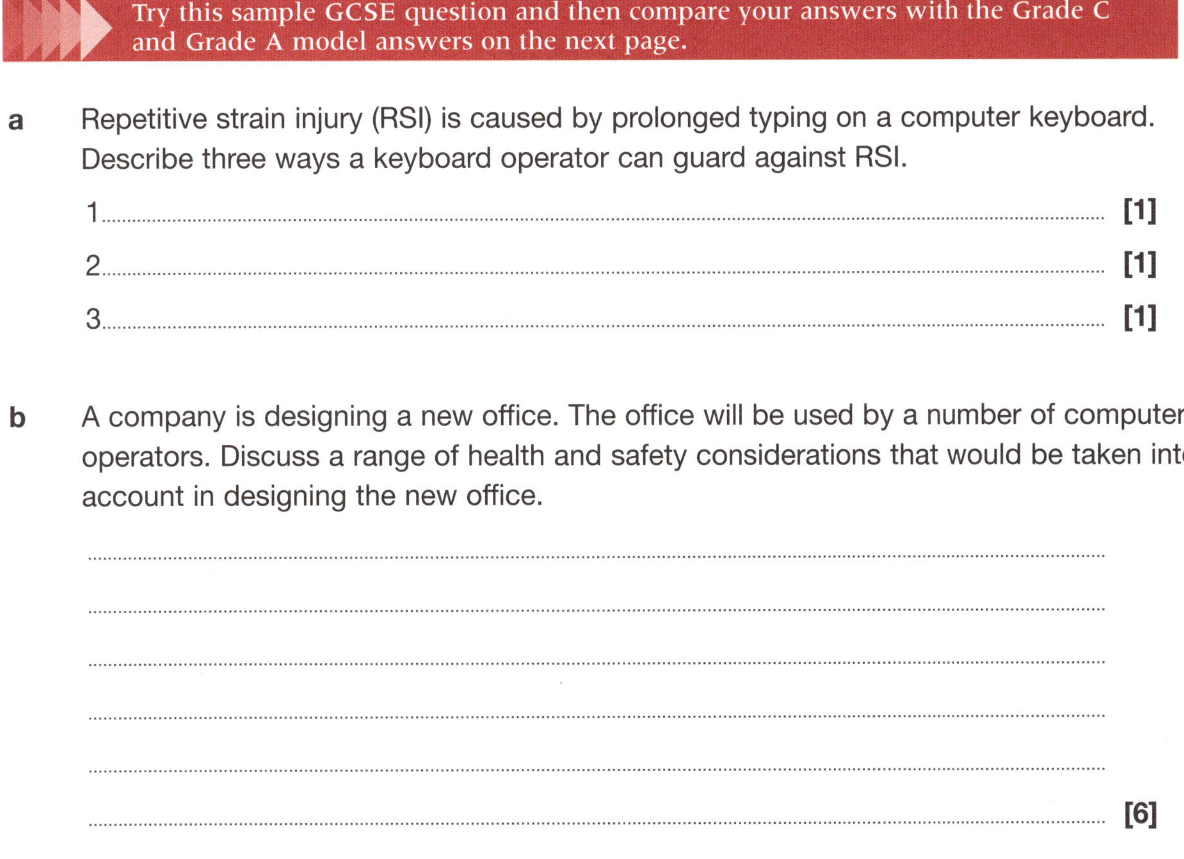

Try this sample GCSE question and then compare your answers with the Grade C and Grade A model answers on the next page.

a   Repetitive strain injury (RSI) is caused by prolonged typing on a computer keyboard. Describe three ways a keyboard operator can guard against RSI.

1. .... **[1]**

2. .... **[1]**

3. .... **[1]**

b   A company is designing a new office. The office will be used by a number of computer operators. Discuss a range of health and safety considerations that would be taken into account in designing the new office.

....

....

....

....

....

.... **[6]**

(Total 9 marks)

These two answers are at grades C and A. Compare which one your answer is closest to and think how you could have improved it.

GRADE C ANSWER

Amy has correctly identified the importance of positioning the keyboard, but answers like 'do not use the keyboard too much', whilst effective at reducing the chance of RSI, would not be much help to a keyboard operator. Sitting correctly is simply repeating the importance of correct position, which has already gained a mark. One mark awarded.

Only two marks awarded as the candidate has not fully explained why these points are required and some of the points are irrelevant.

AMY

a Try not to use the keyboard too much. Position the keyboard correctly. ✓ Sit correctly in your chair.

b The company would want lots of power points so the computers could be plugged in. ✓ People like to work in air-conditioned environments and windows are important. Letting sunlight in will help a good working atmosphere. Carpets should not be made of man-made fibres. ✓ People like to have lots of room to move about.

4 marks = Grade C answer

Grade booster ⋯⟩ move a C to a B

Try to cover each point systematically. Do not repeat the same point using different words. Number your points. Think about the questions. They ask for health and safety considerations. Do not waste time describing what people might like, rather than what they need.

GRADE A ANSWER

Three marks awarded.

A good answer with good justification made for each point. Six marks awarded.

FLO

a Use a keyboard with good ergonomic design to avoid unnecessary movement. ✓ Make sure that your typing technique is good, and position the keyboard correctly. ✓ Take regular breaks away from the keyboard. ✓

b It is important to ensure that there are enough power sockets ✓ so that sockets are not overloaded, causing a fire risk. ✓ Ample sockets also ensure that cables do not have to be trailed all over the office. ✓ Although people like windows that they can look out of, sunlight produces glare on screens, so blinds should be fitted. ✓ Computers are affected by static electricity ✓ so man-made fibres should be avoided in furnishings like chair covers and carpets. ✓

9 marks = Grade A answer

Grade booster ⋯⟩ move A to A*

Answer clearly and use examples where this will help to show the examiner what you want to say. It does not hurt to give more examples than asked for in the question, providing you have sufficient time. Read through all your answers when you have finished the examination and correct or expand on answers where you think it will help.

Short-answer questions

1 Which of the following health problems have been identified as having a link with prolonged use of computers?

A backache

B influenza

C headaches

D athletes foot

E skin rashes

F brain tumours

G tennis elbow ③

2 Eye strain can be avoided by which of the following steps?

A wearing glasses

B looking away from the screen regularly

C positioning the screen correctly

D positioning the screen close to the operator

E positioning the screen far away from the operator ②

Long-answer questions

1 a) Describe **two** precautions that must be taken to ensure that an office using computers is a **safe environment** in which to work.

Precaution 1 .... ①

Precaution 2 .... ①

b) Describe **two** actions that computer operators should take to protect their own health and safety while at work.

Action 1 .... ①

Action 2 .... ①

TOTAL 4

2 Describe the steps that a computer operator should take to avoid eye problems.

....

.... ②

TOTAL 2

3 State **three** health and safety points that the law requires employers to put in place to protect workers using computer systems.

Point 1 .... ①

Point 2 .... ①

Point 3 .... ①

TOTAL 3

4 The law protecting workers using computer systems lays down a number of minimum requirements for computer systems and furniture. All new furniture and equipment must meet these standards. Describe **four** of the standards.

Standard 1 .... ③

Standard 2 .... ③

Standard 3 .... ③

Standard 4 .... ③

TOTAL 12

5 Name **four** health problems that can occur when working with computers for long periods of time.

Problem 1 .... ①

Problem 2 .... ①

Problem 3 .... ①

Problem 4 .... ①

TOTAL 4

QUESTION BANK ANSWERS

Short-answer questions

❶ A, C, E

❷ B, E

Long-answer questions

❶ a) One mark for each answer of any two from the following: smoke alarm; no trailing cables; electrical safety; monitors positioned correctly; correct positions of chairs and desks. **❷**

EXAMINER'S TIP

Although there is only one mark for each answer, the question asks you to describe, not state, the precautions. You will not gain marks with one-word answers.

b) One mark for each answer of any two from the following: take regular breaks away from the monitor; look away from the screen regularly; take regular exercise; maintain correct posture while seated; sit at a suitable distance from the screen. **❷**

EXAMINER'S TIP

The second part of this question relates to the user, not the company. You must not repeat answers given for the first part of the question, as these will not gain any marks.

❷ Have regular eye checks. Look away from the screen, at a distant object, regularly. **❷**

❸ Inspections, training, job design, eye tests. **❸**

EXAMINER'S TIP

The question asks you to state, *not* explain.

❹ Display screens should not have flicker, must tilt and swivel, must be positioned so there is no reflection of sunlight, and the brightness and contrast should be adjustable. **❸**
Keyboards must be separate from screens, and tiltable, should be easy to use, and the surface of the keyboard should be matt to avoid glare. **❸**

Desks must be large enough to take the computer and paperwork, must not reflect light, and should be situated to avoid unnecessary head movements. **❸**
Chairs must be adjustable and comfortable, and should be provided with a footrest if a worker asks for one. They should allow freedom of movement. **❸**

EXAMINER'S TIP

This question asks you to describe four standards, and is marked out of 12. The examiner therefore requires three points for each standard. Try to select the most common parts of the standards. Although things like heat, humidity and radiation are included in the standards, it is very difficult to draw out three clear points from these to gain the marks. The areas you choose have a clear bearing on the difficulty of the question. Although the examiner asks you to name the areas, no marks are awarded for this. It just helps the examiner to see the relevance of the points you have made.

❺ RSI, backache, eye strain, headache, skin rashes. **❹**

<table>
<tr><td>Centre number</td></tr>
<tr><td>Candidate number</td></tr>
<tr><td>Surname and initials</td></tr>
</table>

Letts Examining Group

General Certificate of Secondary Education

ICT

Foundation and Higher combined

<table>
<tr><td colspan="2">For Examiner's use only</td></tr>
<tr><td>Section A
1-27</td><td></td></tr>
<tr><td>Section B
1-17</td><td></td></tr>
<tr><td>Total</td><td></td></tr>
</table>

You should answer all questions

Time: Section A   30 minutes

Section B   60 minutes

Instructions to candidates

Write your name in the space provided.

You should attempt all short answer questions (1–27) before moving on to Section B of this examination paper.

1 You would find the letters QWERTY on a:

   A mouse
   B UK keyboard
   C numeric keypad
   D French keyboard [1]

2 Which of the following items would be used to store data?

   A robotic arm
   B monitor
   C floppy disk
   D plotter [1]

3 The input device that can be used for marking a multiple-choice test is called a:

   A mouse
   B bar code reader
   C OCR reader
   D optical mark reader. [1]

4 The input device used in a supermarket to scan in the prices of goods is called a:

   A mouse
   B bar code reader
   C optical mark reader
   D digitiser. [1]

5 You would you find a magnetic strip on a:

   A credit card
   B keyboard
   C smart card
   D cheque. [1]

6 Which of the following is a pointing device used for computer input?

   A touch screen
   B hard disk
   C CD-ROM drive
   D floppy drive [1]

7 What are you most likely to use when playing computer games?

   A touch screen
   B light pen
   C joystick
   D scanner [1]

[turn over

8 A digitising tablet can be used for:

A printing leaflets
B outputting pictures
C reading bar codes
D tracing diagrams and drawings. **[1]**

9 The term **hard copy** is used in ICT to describe:

A writing on a hard board
B printed output
C storing information on the hard disk
D using a CD-ROM. **[1]**

10 The individual dots that make up a picture on the monitor screen are called:

A coloured spots
B pixies
C dotters
D pixels. **[1]**

11 Factory production lines can be automated by using:

A printers
B CAM
C plotters
D mice. **[1]**

12 What would you use with a flatbed plotter?

A a pen
B toner
C eraser
D roll feeder **[1]**

13 The ink in an ink jet printer is stored in a:

A cartridge
B drum
C ribbon
D bottle. **[1]**

14 The amount of data that a disk can contain is known as:

A volume
B width
C storage capacity
D height. **[1]**

15 A CD-R is:

A read only
B write only
C read and write once
D read and write many times. [1]

16 Formatting a hard disk results in all the data being:

A deleted from the disk
B copied from the disk
C saved to the disk
D reformatted into a different file format. [1]

17 Which two of these items will contain personal data?

A car park ticket
B keyboard
C hospital patient record
D floor turtle
E driving licence
F printer [2]

18 You need to keep a database of your friends' names, addresses and dates of birth, etc. Which of the following ways would be the best way of doing this?

A scraps of paper
B a database
C a spreadsheet
D an address book [1]

19 Say whether the statements are TRUE (T) or FALSE (F).

- Data on floppy disks can be destroyed by magnets. [1]
- A CD-ROM can store more data than a floppy disk. [1]
- Spreadsheet packages are used to create newspapers. [1]
- A modem is used to communicate using the telephone system. [1]
- A school newspaper could be created using DTP. [1]
- Disks must be formatted before they are used. [1]
- Computers are not any good at mathematical calculations. [1]
- A field in a database is used to store all data about one person. [1]
- Spreadsheets use formulae to perform calculations. [1]
- You can use a database to model financial data. [1]

[turn over

Letts

20 Name the parts of the network labelled below.

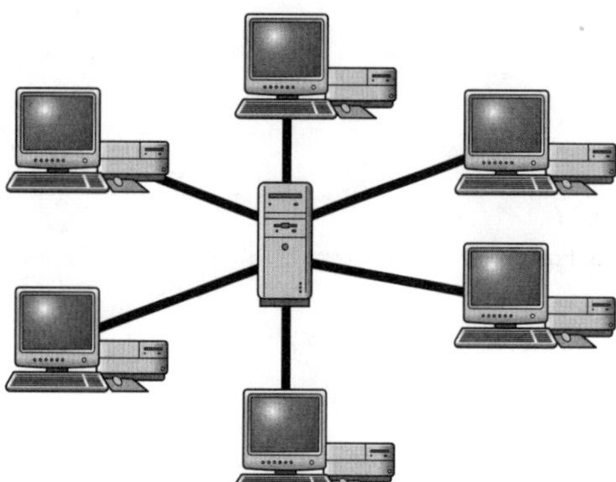

[2]

21 Name the labelled parts in the document shown below.

The day is long, the day is short. It is raining cats and dogs. The wind is blowing hard. You are going to pass this exam because you are revising hard. The day is long, the day is short. It is raining cats and dogs. The wind is blowing hard. You are going to pass this exam because you are revising hard. The day is long, the day is short. It is raining cats and dogs. The wind is blowing hard. You are going to pass this exam because you are revising hard.

Name.........................

Name.........................

Name.........................

Name.........................

Page 3

[4]

22 Define the following terms.

Line spacing

.... [2]

Font type

.... [2]

Font size

.... [2]

Two-column layout

.... [2]

23 Which storage device cannot be erased?

    A CD-ROM

    B floppy disk

    C magnetic tape storage

    D hard disk   **[1]**

24 Indicate which of the following devices are input devices:

    A keyboard

    B mouse

    C printer

    D touch screen

    E monitor

    F digital camera

    G scanner

    H speaker.   **[5]**

25 Feedback can be described as:

    A a computer model

    B a loud noise

    C an output from a system that is used to influence subsequent input

    D an output from a system involving a printer.   **[1]**

26 The process of data capture could involve:

    A looking at printed output

    B entering, processing and printing results

    C collection, verification and input

    D collection, entering data and validation.   **[1]**

27 Data can be collected in a computer-controlled system using:

    A a printer

    B multiple choice forms

    C a keyboard

    D a sensor.   **[1]**

(Total 52 marks)

[turn over

Section B: Long-answer questions

1 A graphic artist wishes to include images in a magazine. **Compare** the following methods of collecting the images: Clipart, scanning, drawing the images themselves.

....

....

....

....

....

....

....

.... **[8]**

2 The manager of a video shop decides to send a standard letter to all his customers.

(a) State what the term **standard letter** means.

.... **[1]**

(b) The video shop manager uses two pieces of software: a database and a word processor. Describe how the manager will produce and print the letters using this software.

....

....

....

....

....

.... **[6]**

3 Allbright Jewellers uses a computer-controlled alarm system to protect its shop against theft.

(a) Name **one** suitable input device for the alarm system.

.... **[1]**

(b) Name **one** suitable output device for the alarm system.

.... **[1]**

(c) Explain how the burglar alarm system will work.

....

....

....

.... **[4]**

4 Bob Daley is a self-employed painter and decorator. At the moment Bob stores all of his records using a paper-based filing system.

(a) Give **two** drawbacks of storing important information in a paper-based filing system.

Drawback 1

.... **[1]**

Drawback 2

.... **[1]**

(b) Give **two** drawbacks of using a computer to store the information.

Drawback 1

.... **[1]**

Drawback 2

.... **[1]**

5 Sue Grabbit works as a writer for a magazine. She uses a word processor to write her articles. Sue spends most of her working day using the computer.

(a) Give **two** features of word-processing software that make it suitable for this task.

Feature 1

.... **[1]**

Feature 2

.... **[1]**

(b) Identify **two** health problems that could result from continued use of a computer.

Problem 1

.... **[1]**

Problem 2

.... **[1]**

[turn over

(c) For **each** problem you identified in **(b)** give **one** method of reducing the health risks.

Problem 1

....

.... **[2]**

Problem 2

....

.... **[2]**

6   Malcolm Manley has a bank account with the National Eastminster Bank. The bank has given Malcolm a cheque book, an automatic telling machine (ATM) card and a debit card. The bank also has an internet banking facility.

(a) Give **three** items of data that are pre-printed on every cheque in a chequebook.

Item 1 .... **[1]**

Item 2 .... **[1]**

Item 3 .... **[1]**

(b) Some of this information is printed using MICR.

   (i) What do the letters MICR stand for?

.... **[1]**

   (ii) State **one** benefit to the bank of using MICR.

.... **[1]**

(c) Explain how Malcolm can use his ATM card to withdraw cash from the bank.

....

....

....

....

.... **[5]**

(d) What are the benefits to the **bank** of an internet banking service?

....

....

....

.... **[4]**

(e) Give **two** methods the bank could use to ensure that only authorised account holders can access the data held on the internet banking service.

Method 1

.... **[1]**

Method 2

.... **[1]**

7 An estate agent collects data about people who are intending to buy houses. The data is stored on a computer database.

(a) Explain **three** restrictions that the Data Protection Act places on this data.

Restriction 1

.... **[1]**

Restriction 2

.... **[1]**

Restriction 3

.... **[1]**

(b) The estate agent has a web site where it displays information about current properties.

Identify **one** way that the Copyright, Design and Patents Act protects the information held on the web site.

.... **[1]**

(c) A customer enters the estate agent's shop and finds it empty. A computer is switched on and is displaying a list of files.

(i) Which law makes it illegal for the customer to view files on the computer?

.... **[1]**

(ii) Give **one** other restriction that this law places on computer users.

.... **[1]**

[turn over

8 A theatre has an on-line booking system on its web site. Customers can use the system to book tickets. The system displays a list of unsold seats. When a customer makes a booking this list is updated immediately.

Which type of processing is used by the booking system?

.... **[1]**

9 Give **two** differences between a CD-ROM and a floppy disk.

Difference 1

.... **[1]**

Difference 2

.... **[1]**

10 Kevin Scratchly wants to design a new logo for his local swimming team. He is unsure whether to create a bitmap or a vector image.

(a) What is a bitmap image?

....

.... **[2]**

(b) What is a vector image?

....

.... **[2]**

11 Maggie Might uses macros to help her save time when using her computer.

(a) What is a macro?

....

.... **[2]**

(b) Give an example of when Maggie might use a macro.

.... **[1]**

(c) Maggie has created a keyboard short-cut to help her run her macro.

What is a keyboard short-cut?

....

.... **[2]**

12 The following table is an extract from a database of pupil information kept by a school.

LAST	FIRST	JOINED	FORM	ADMISSION NUMBER
Henry	Freddie	1-9-1998	JP	23467
Smith	Paul	1-9-1997	WH	21345
Burns	Marcia	1-9-1999	CH	23556
Fernandez	Mario	1-9-1998	CH	32446

(a) Which field is the primary key field?

.... **[1]**

(b) Why is this field the primary key field?

.... **[1]**

(c) Give **one** occasion when a record might be added to the database.

.... **[1]**

(d) Give **one** occasion when a record might be deleted from the database.

.... **[1]**

(e) Give **one** occasion when a record might be amended.

.... **[1]**

13 Discuss the social implications of the increased use of the internet.

....

....

....

....

....

....

.... **[7]**

[turn over

14 What are the implications of an increasing number of people using their computers to work from home?

....

....

....

....

....

....

.... **[7]**

15 What are the economic implications of an increased use of computer technology to manufacture products?

....

....

....

....

.... **[5]**

16 (a) A modern aircraft is controlled by a system called 'fly by wire'. Explain the term fly by wire.

....

....

....

....

....

.... **[6]**

(b) A fly by wire system uses real-time processing. Explain why this is important.

....

.... **[2]**

17 State **one** situation where automatic data logging equipment is commonly used.

.... **[1]**

(Total 100 marks)

Answers to mock examination

Section A

1	B	[1]
2	C	[1]
3	D	[1]
4	B	[1]
5	A	[1]
6	A	[1]
7	C	[1]
8	D	[1]
9	B	[1]
10	B	[1]
11	B	[1]
12	A	[1]
13	A	[1]
14	C	[1]
15	C	[1]
16	A	[1]
17	C and E	[2]
18	B	[1]
19	T, T, F, T, T, T, F, F, T, F	[10]
20	A=Client and B=Server	[2]
21	Left margin, header, right margin, footer	[4]

22 Line spacing is the amount of space between two lines of text – sometimes also called leading. Font type is the style of lettering, e.g. Times New Roman. Font size is how big the lettering is, measured in points. The higher the point size the bigger the lettering, hence font size. Two-column layout means the page is divided vertically into two columns. [8]

23	A	[1]
24	A, B, D, F, G	[1]
25	C	[1]

26 Option D – collection entering data and validation [1]

27 D [1]

Section B

1 Marks are awarded for mentioning the following points, up to a maximum of four marks for each method.

Clipart: cheap and freely available; copyright free; large amount of images available to select from; can save a lot of time compared to other methods. Disadvantages include that your publication may look the same as a lot of others; you may not be able to find exactly the right image; you may still have copyright problems as many Clipart images are only freely usable if what you are producing is not going to be published.

Scanning: possible to copy any material; can be used for text and images; fast way of gaining images and text. Disadvantages are cost of the scanner; amount of memory available in computer; images that are sometimes too big; you also have to be careful to avoid copyright problems.

Self-drawn images: you get exactly what you want; you have to be skilled to draw the images; you need the right software; drawing the pictures can take a long time. [8]

> **EXAMINER'S TIP**
>
> *Think about the needs of a graphic artist before you answer this question. The question asks you to compare, so you should give advantages and disadvantages for each system of image capture, compared with each other.*

2 a) A large amount of the data that the letter contains will be the same, whichever customer it is being sent to, with only details such as name and address being different. [1]

   b) He/she will type the letter using the word processor, setting up a template with markers for name and address and any other personal details. He/she will link these markers to a database so that mail merge can add the customer personal details. They will then print out each letter. [6]

3 a) One mark for any of the following: noise sensor, pressure sensor, (body) heat sensor, infra-red beam. [1]

   b) One mark for any of the following: loudspeaker, siren, data-link to a control centre, telephone link to police station. [1]

   c) The input device collects data from the shop. It sends this data to the processor. The processor compares the data to the target levels it has been programmed with. If the data is outside tolerance, the processor switches on the output device. [4]

4 a) Takes up a lot of room. Paper might go missing. Difficult to analyse the information. **[2]**

b) Computer is expensive to buy. Will need training in how to use it. Records can be deleted/data can get corrupted. **[2]**

EXAMINER'S TIP

Where there is only one mark, try to be succinct, using specific ICT terms, such as data corruption, information needs, etc.

5 a) Can enter/edit text. Can use the spell-check/grammar check facility. **[2]**

b) Repetitive strain injury (RSI) or upper limb disorder (ULD); eye strain/headaches; back problems. **[2]**

c) RSI/ULD: take regular breaks, finger exercises, look away from the screen. Eye strain/headaches: regular breaks, good lighting, anti-glare screen filter. Back problems: better chair, better posture, walk or regular exercise. **[4]**

6 a) Any three from: account number, sort-code, customer name, bank name and address. **[3]**

b) i) Magnetic Ink Character Recognition. **[1]**

ii) Any one from: quicker to read the data; less chance of error than with a human operator. **[1]**

c) Any five from: Malcolm inserts his ATM card into an ATM. His account information is read from the magnetic strip on the card. He enters his Personal Identification Number (PIN) into the machine. His PIN is verified against the number stored on the card. He enters the amount of cash to be withdrawn. The ATM checks with the bank that there are sufficient funds in the account. If there are, the ATM counts and issues the requested cash. **[5]**

d) Any four from: Fewer branches are needed. Fewer staff are needed. This reduces costs (overheads). Customers can print their own statements. This reduces paper costs at the bank. The bank can become more competitive. The bank can reach more customers in areas where it did not previously have branches. **[4]**

e) Issue customers with user names and passwords. Use data encryption software. **[2]**

EXAMINER'S TIP

This type of question is harder than it looks at first, as it asks for knowledge about the use of a cheque book and bank. You might not be familiar with these concepts if you are still at school. In order to answer the question correctly, it is important to think through security and other data needs involved in banking.

7 a) Any three from:
The data must be accurate. The data must be up to date. The data must only be used for the purpose for which it was collected. The data must be deleted when it is no longer required. The estate agent should protect the data against theft, loss or corruption. **[3]**

EXAMINER'S TIP

Even though only one mark is awarded for each answer, the question asks you to explain. You will not get a mark in this instance for a one word answer, but will need to use a simple sentence to gain the mark available.

b) Information must not be copied from the web site and used without the permission of the estate agent. **[1]**

c) i) Computer Misuse Act. **[1]**

ii) One from: illegal to delete files without authorisation; illegal to copy files without authorisation; illegal to alter files without authorisation. **[1]**

8 Real-time processing. **[1]**

EXAMINER'S TIP

Both batch and real time processing methods can be used in many situations. The question gives you the answer by stating that the booking system must be updated immediately.

9 A CD-ROM can hold more data than a floppy disk. A floppy disk can have new data written to it, a CD-ROM cannot. **[2]**

EXAMINER'S TIP

The answer is given in the question if you think through the terms and their meaning. CD-ROM stands for Read Only Memory.

10 a) Any two from the following: A bitmap image is made up of individual dots or pixels. Each individual dot can be edited or deleted. As a result, a lot of memory is needed to store the image. **[2]**

b) Any two from the following: A vector image contains data in the form of a mathematical model about the properties of each shape in the image. For example, a red square block is stored as an equation for the block and an instruction for the colour inside the block. **[2]**

EXAMINER'S TIP

Logos have to be rescaled, so a vector image is important.

11 a) A sequence of commands that have been saved by the computer. [2]

b) One from the following: When opening a template such as a letter file. When entering standard information onto a letter, such as a block of text. When carrying out a routine, such as saving a document in a particular folder. [1]

c) It is an instruction to the computer to carry out a specific action when a combination of keys is depressed at the same time (e.g. ALT + L). [2]

12 a) ADMISSION NUMBER. [1]

b) It is the key field because no two pupils can have the same admission number. [1]

c) A record might be added when a pupil joins the school. [1]

d) A record might be deleted when a pupil leaves the school. [1]

e) A record might be amended when a pupil changes class. [1]

13 Any seven points from the following: Health risks of increased computer use; spread of viruses; access to unsuitable material; less personal social contact; more contact with people via discussion groups etc.; problems with people infiltrating chat rooms; reliance on computer technology; greater ability to buy goods from home; greater ability to work from home. [7]

14 Any seven points from the following: Spend less time commuting; more time with family; can plan when to do the work; isolation from work colleagues; may feel vulnerable and unable to resist work demands; do not have to live near to office; need to have a work area/study within the home; may cost more – heating/lighting, etc. [7]

15 Any five points from the following: Robots replace human workers; increased unemployment amongst humans; products may become cheaper if more efficiently produced; fewer manufacturing jobs needed; more jobs needed to build the robots; manufacturing job roles change – now need to supervise the robots, not perform the tasks. [5]

16 a) 'Fly by wire' means that the pilot uses a computer input device, rather than manual mechanically linked controls, to instruct a computer to control the output devices, e.g. flaps, and other mechanical devices. This type of system helps to monitor and correct any pilot error and also lightens the amount of force needed on the controls. [6]

b) This is important because the action must occur at the exact time required by the pilot. Timing is vital for the plane to fly. [2]

17 One mark for stating any of the following, or similar: weather station, traffic monitoring system, scientific experiment monitoring, speed cameras, hospital bedside. [1]

Index